The Exile of Britney Spears

For Hannah, Isabelle, Charlotte, Agnes, Charlotte Eudora, and Alice

Stay strong little ladies

The Exile of Britney Spears

A Tale of 21st Century Consumption

Christopher R. Smit

intellect Bristol, UK / Chicago, USA

First published in the UK in 2011 by
Intellect, The Mill, Parnall Road, Fishponds, Bristol, BS16 3JG, UK

First published in the USA in 2011 by
Intellect, The University of Chicago Press, 1427 E. 60th Street,
Chicago, IL 60637, USA

A catalogue record for this book is available from the British Library.

Cover designer: Holly Rose
Copy-editor: Rebecca Vaughan Williams
Typesetting: Mac Style, Beverley, E. Yorkshire

ISBN 978-1-84150-410-0

Printed and bound by Gutenberg Press, Malta.

Contents

Acknowledgments

This book was a risk to write, and I wish to give thanks to those who saw it as worthwhile. To my friend Helen Sterk, many thanks for your support, defence and critical eye. Furthermore, to my colleagues Craig Hanson, Susan Felch, Adam Wolpa, William Romanowski, Carl Plantinga, James Vanden Bosch, Claudia Beversluis, Matt Walhout and Dan Garcia, thank you so much for your words of advice, time and attention. Thanks also to Marissa Christy for copyediting the first draft.

To my friends Ken Heffner, Erin O'Conner, David Dark, Rob and Kirstin Vander Geissen-Rietsma, Leo Van Arragon, Joan VanDessel, Steve D., Christy Prins, Benjamin Van Arragon, Melanie Morrison, Scott and Michelle Millen, Mike and Cheri Cornell and those of you caught unexpectedly in conversations about digestion metaphors, thanks for talking and listening.

Many of my students helped me with this book, by either reading early editions of it, or by assisting me with research tasks. To the book's first readers, Chaz Amidon, Aaron Roorda, Jon derNederlanden, Arlen Eldridge and Lindsay Makowski, rock on. And to Katie Baker and Taylor Swart, thanks for being my hands and arms.

To the staff of Intellect Books, particularly May Yao and Jelena Stanovik, many thanks for your support, advice and wit.

And finally, to Lisa and our son: my fondness for you both will never be shifted. Thanks for letting me obsess. Love you.

Preface

Two Notes for Readers

This book contains fifteen critical observations about the life and career of Britney Jean Spears. Through these observations, I will offer an interpretation of the way culture, media, spectacle, gender and embodiment work together to create some startling realities for us and her. While you are reading, it will be helpful to keep the following two notes in mind.

First, this is not a history of Britney Spears. This is not a biographical account of her life nor is it intended to be at all finite. Rather, it is creative interpretation, the criticism bathed in the rapid manner most of us come across images of and stories about Britney – it has been written employing primarily digital media. As such, it is presented in a fashion that mirrors our consumption of Britney Spears: quick, Internet-based, at times alarming, at other times filled with random context. The information found in the chapters could have been found by you. In fact, much of it probably was at one time. I simply collected it all, rearranged it and re-represented it. When necessary, I have included notes on further reading at the end of the book.

Second, this book is an accusation. I have assumed that the breaking of Britney Spears has been, is and will continue to be an act of collective behaviour.[1] She is involved, certainly. But more importantly, I conclude that our consumption, exiling and re-welcoming of Britney has been detrimental because none of us are innocent. I make this point early on in the book because I want us to think differently about what has happened to her. In the end, the reader must decide whether he or she will admit to complicit behaviour in her destruction and reconstruction.

Most importantly, that reader must also know that I am accusing myself here. I have a full understanding of the fact that the words written in this book can be construed as further exploitation of Britney Spears. My hope is that by admitting my own involvement in her fall that I might possibly lessen any further objectification.

Christopher R. Smit
Grand Rapids, Michigan
July 2010

Note

1. To highlight this collective responsibility and action you will note that I often use the pronoun 'we' to identify complicit behaviours exhibited in the act of consumption. Some who read this book will find such a word highly presumptuous, feeling that they are far removed from the group of people who actively pursued and 'broke' Britney Spears. It is precisely this reaction that causes me to use communal language; if you participate at all in new media platforms like Facebook, MySpace or Twitter, if you catch yourself reading with interest the tabloid headlines in grocery store checkout lines, use electronic media to perform daily tasks, watch television entertainment news, speak to friends or colleagues about celebrity gossip or are a fan of any popular culture icon, then you are part of the system that I am accusing in this book. In other words, you do not need to be a fan of Britney Spears in order to participate in electronic, digital, mediated exile. By using such systems, I would argue, we validate both their benefits and their pitfalls.

Prologue

Waiting

We were waiting for Britney Spears, that's the easiest way to put it. She was predicted to us years ago, a ghost waiting to happen. The fortune-teller was not behind curtains, engrossed by the sweet aroma of scented candles, bathed in light filtered by scarves, tucked deep inside the tent at Coney Island. It wasn't that mysterious at all. The fortune-teller was in our living room, plain as day. The fortune-teller was folded up on our end table, tucked under coffee cups. She was centered in the family room, turned on by us in the evening to watch Ed Sullivan. The fortune-teller was down the road, smelling of popcorn, showing us magical images on a bigger than life screen. The fortune-teller was in our cars, playing us rock 'n' roll music on Friday night, ministers on Sunday morning. We played records on the fortune-teller, eight tracks, cassettes. The fortune-teller was everywhere, mediating our world.

The media was giving us a glimpse of Britney Jean Spears. Of what she could become, of what we could become.

The would-be Britney was everywhere and nowhere at the same time. She was conscious and unconscious, present and absent, in front of us and yet still behind us. The apparition, the possibility of Britney was the fortune, the future of us. She would become a symbol of decadence, of good gone bad, of purity, of pleasure, and pain. The text of Britney Spears, body and soul, had been played and performed for years before it was actually visible, touchable.

We see the text of Britney in the tale of Marilyn Monroe. In the magazines that published the latter's picture, the movie studios who put her on the silver screen, and the gossip columnists who chipped their way into her life, we see the beginnings of the story that would become Britney. Ernesto Cardenal's 'Prayer for Marilyn Monroe' maps it all out for us – the destruction of a young woman by the media giants.[1] Killers, no other way to describe them. But therein lies the difference between the downfall of Marilyn Monroe and that of Britney Spears. Who participated in the destruction, who was complicit in the action of death for Britney? Who exiled her?

Marilyn was consumed from a distance, one manifested by print journalism and the original channels of telecommunications. The radio, the magazine, the film, the newspaper, these were the avenues we drove on to get to her. We were not driving however. We were just along for the ride. The consumer, happy and sleepy in the backseat.

However, by the late 1990s, when Britney was making her debut, we were swiftly becoming the producers of the mediated world. Consider that by 1996, thanks to cheap technology and widespread access, the following were in our hands: almost professional video and audio production technology, websites, e-mail, digital photography, cellular telephones, independent publishing and digital networks. Regulation aside, which in the late 1990s meant very little anyway, the consumer/producer of media was gaining a new social capacity, a new source of power. And this was a power felt not only in the digital world but also the real world. For a lesson in this, remember Rodney King. Specifically, bring to mind the images captured on video by onlookers of those policeman beating him. Jackasses before the show was ever produced by Johnny Knoxville and MTV.

These videos of Rodney King being beaten for the first time captured a new synergy between the physical and the simulated, between sensual and digital. More importantly, there was a new connection between the life being tasted, felt and heard by one man, the life being video recorded by the onlooker, and then viewed by the consequently riotous masses. Evidence of a new kind of reality, one that wasn't just represented, but one that transcended into the place where the blow of a nightstick could do real harm to all us. In other words, where media became corporeal.

The difference between the baby boomer generation and generation X or Y, or the millennials, the net generation, or whatever, is that the former watched media where the latter groups desire to be part of it.[2] Really, it's more than desire. It's not that we want to be a part of the mediated hemisphere, it's that we feel that we are entitled to be a part of it. For so many years 'they' have been dancing in front of us, Johnny Carson, Tom Brokaw, Walter Cronkite, Jack Benny, Merv Griffin, Dick Clark, Dick Van Dyke. The women are there too – Mary Tyler Moore, Barbara Walters, Lucille Ball. We had been the beneficiaries, the takers. Then, in 1973, documentary filmmakers Alan and Susan Raymond introduced us to the Loud family on PBS. And we heard them. In their film *An American Family* the Raymonds told us that the everyday could be spectacular.[3] That the ordinary could be extraordinary. That we could climb inside the magic mirror with Alice. It wasn't just about *them* anymore.

The deal was sealed in 1992. In that year MTV aired its first season of *The Real World*. Seven strangers, living together, making history, blurring the lines between reality and fantasy, foreshadowing a new cultural moment.[4] The idea of 'realness' had always been questioned by philosophers, theologians, academics. Never, however, had it been placed inside the daily conversations, thoughts and musings of us. Unconsciously or consciously (it doesn't matter), we as a culture were placing the idea of reality on the chopping block. We were discovering a new mode of living, one far outside the privy of anthropologists. We had discovered an alternative reality, a place in which avatars freely roam, in which Andy Warhol's fifteen minutes expanded into infinity.

Today, my students use the word *blogosphere* when they refer to the matrix of information, opinion and technology of the digital landscape. This is actually an incorrect descriptor –

what they are referring to is much larger than entries in a blog, much more important, much more culturally significant. But that doesn't seem to matter much to them, and why should it? They know what they're talking about. It's me that needs to catch up. All of us actually need to catch up. It's the word 'sphere' that should make us pause. I use the word the way Max Weber did, as an all-encompassing context of life, as a container within which action becomes meaningful.[5] What if we all used the word that way? What if we all understood the digital sphere as a cultural context? To do that would be to admit that the ways in which we make meaning are created and maintained within a world that is primarily invisible. Digital life, invisible life.

How far can we push this metaphor? Can we extend it back 50 years, 75 years? Can it be applied to the history of media itself? As we survey the arrival of scribal technology, the printing press, the optical and electrical telegraph, radio, the cinema, television, of all telecommunications, can we sense the creation of a new sphere of meaning, one that is relatively far from our field of vision yet deeply embedded in our perception? If it is possible to suggest that all media has been invisible, then it is also possible to suggest that we have been, are, and will always be unconscious players in a game that we know very little about.[6]

The chapters of this book reject this last suggestion. We are not simply pawns being moved around a plane of meaning and value, manipulated and articulated by those who run the media world. We are part of the project. Moreover, the way we experience and feel the world around us is beginning to be guided, translated, even dictated, by the things we do with electronic, digital and communicative devices. If we send out hateful messages to a classmate on Facebook, they might just become evidence in an investigation of a real life death. The virtual and the real, together at last.

The more succinctly we understand this, the easier it becomes to comprehend – living in the digital world involves more than simple observation. By writing in blogs, surfing the web, chatting with friends on Skype, downloading MP3s, watching television on websites (legally or otherwise), consuming pornography from websites, banking online, contributing to Twitter, Facebook or MySpace, by e-mailing important documents to professors, grading exams online, purchasing books, DVDs, clothing and everything else we want from Amazon, by marketing ourselves and consuming others on dating websites, by doing all the things that fill our busy lives in front of our computer screens and smart phones, we validate a system. We justify a context of meaning. For better or worse, we construct and maintain the digital world that has created a space for Britney Spears.

The longer story is told in the chapters that follow – Britney's creation, our consumption of her, her exile and her second coming. The short story is this. Traditional electronic media, as described above, created a world in which entertainment and information amalgamated into something that we valued. We made time for it, spent money on it, gave it our attention. Along the way, we made media our own system of expression. We began using it as a system of identification. People knew us by the media we spent time with. In other words, we became fans.[7] We congregated with other fanatics who followed the same music we did, the same movies we liked, the same television shows we watched. Media became cultural. It became a part of the way we made sense of our social comings and goings. But it became more than that. It also became psychological. The media wandered its way into our impressions of ourselves. It became indications of who we were and who we wanted to be. The stars, those wonderful people who were nestled inside the medium's message, became conduits for our maturation as individuals. If we could be like *them*, everything in our world would make sense. And thus, it also became physical: diets, tanning booths, haircuts, clothing choices, all became ways that we physically reacted to our new reality.[8]

But fandom would not be enough. Eventually, like in any cultural event, power would become a problem.

In a mediated world, especially one as complicated as ours, the question that inevitably gets to the tips of our tongues is as follows: who has the power to make meaning? Research in postwar America of communication systems centred on this question. Hitler and Goebbels painted wonderful ideological pictures called propaganda. Beautiful manipulation that led to the destruction of human beings. American communications scholars wondered if such beauty and power had a role to play in the movies we watched. And so in the 1950s, while a popular culture was burgeoning, so too was a paranoia about the power of images. But on a less scholarly level, the consciousness of the American media consumer was also considering power. Translated as involvement, these questions of power by Joe and Jane America led to a desire to be part of the project known as the mass media.

Some would have us believe that media desire, in all its forms, is actually just given to us by the media giants. We have no role to play, no volition to exert in what is made popular and what is not. Blue jeans, bubblegum, Batman, these things and many others were not influenced into existence by us. They were given to us, their popularity was manufactured, a perfect illusion of interests.[9] And while this may have its justifications, isn't it more interesting to think that we had a role to play in the creation of the popular? That our desires to be part of the project actually translated into a power of production? That rather than being simply consumers, that we were creators all along?

The creation focused on in this book is female celebrity, particularly Britney Spears. On one level, we could be discussing any of the female celebrities of the last decade – Christina Aguilera, Jessica Simpson, Mandy Moore, Lindsay Lohan, Avril Lavigne, Kelly Clarkson, Hannah Montana/Miley Cyrus or Lady GaGa. All of these women, when looked at with the lens employed by this book, are our creation. This is not to say that the media men (mostly men) did not play a role in their creation, or for that matter the stars themselves. Rather, it is simply to point out that consumers of media are no longer innocent bystanders. We give permission, we take responsibility, we own expression, we play a role in all of these stories. And our roles affect images, representation and the real.

The story of Britney Spears, of her creation, fall and 'comeback', is the quintessential narrative of digital celebrity. She is the perfect text to learn from, the perfect body to criticize, the imperfect life to consider, the one reason to remind ourselves of the ways life can go when we are at the steering wheel.

We were waiting for Britney Spears. She was not waiting for us.

Notes

1. Cardenal's beautiful and haunting poem about Marilyn Monroe creates a good context through which to understand this book in both content and style. Its relationship to this work on Britney Spears is found clearly in the way the poem humanizes female celebrity. If I am able to criticize and honour Britney Spears the way that Cardenal does Marilyn Monroe, then I will have succeeded in my work. Ernesto Cardenal, *Marilyn Monroe and Other Poems*. London: Continuum International, 1975.
2. The exception is, perhaps, game shows. Being a contestant on shows like *Let's Make a Deal* and *The Price is Right* allowed participation for the everyday viewer and consumer of media. However, such 'participation' was only momentary. Of course, contemporary reality television changes this entire scenario wherein 'participation' on a show like, say, *Survivor*, involves not only momentary participation during the taping of the show, but also the cultural capital that comes along with being on the cast of such a popular program.
3. For in-depth analysis of the PBS documentary series *An American Family* see Jeffrey Ruoff, *An American Family: A Televised Life*. Minneapolis: University of Minnesota Press, 2001. Much more than a behind the scenes look at this influential series, Ruoff's work examines the deeper political, cultural and media-related ramifications of representation of everyday life. As he explains, the Loud family offered viewers a way to investigate the experience of class, race and sexuality, the latter of which took centre stage as Lance, the oldest son, was openly gay.
4. So much more can be said about *The Real World* and its influence on the current fascination with, and popularity of, reality television. In my own study of the show I have tried to examine the manner in which 'reality' is manipulated by MTV producers in such a way that it becomes seamlessly fused with other programming on the network. MTV offered the genesis moment of what has come to be termed 'lifestyle programming', through which consumers/viewers are sold particular manners of living alongside actual products. In particular, *The Real World* works in a way that provides consumer/viewers with particular ideologies regarding race, class, sexuality and gender. For more on this discussion see Anthony Enns and Christopher Smit, 'The Creation and Corruption of Diversity in MTV's *The Real World*', *Studies and Popular Culture* 22.1 (1999): 15–26.
5. Max Weber employed the word 'sphere' in many of his writings as a way of partitioning certain elements of social experience. The following definition clarifies its usefulness in our current project: 'According to Weber, the life of the individual as well as society itself can be conceptualized as consisting of separate spheres or orders, which tend to become more autonomous overtime. These spheres are often in conflict with one another; they are also governed by a certain autonomy and have an inner logic of their own.' Richard Swedberg, ed., *Max Weber: Essays in Economic Sociology*. Princeton: Princeton University Press, 1999, p. 271.
6. For more on the social history of media, in particular the ways in which media create and maintain our realities see Asa Briggs and Peter Burke, *A Social History of the Media: From Gutenberg to the Internet*. Cambridge: Polity Press, 2005.
7. Much of my thinking about fandom is inspired by the work of Henry Jenkins. Easily the world's expert on the ways media consumers have become media producers, Jenkins' work with new media provides an illustrious and informative context for our work here. For more reading see Henry Jenkins, *Fans, Bloggers, and Gamers: Exploring Participatory Culture*. New York: New York University Press, 2006.
8. Literature on stardom, celebrity and the cultural/political effect of each, is expansive. I will point to several of the studies that have influenced my thinking throughout this book, though encourage

the interested reader to dig further according to specific media interests. For more on celebrity and stardom see P. David Marshall, *Celebrity and Power: Fame in Contemporary Culture*. 4th ed. Minneapolis: University of Minnesota Press, 2004; Graem Turner, *Understanding Celebrity*. Thousand Oaks: Sage Publications, 2004; David Giles, *Illusions of Immortality: A Psychology of Fame and Celebrity*. New York: St Martin's Press, 2000; Joshua Gamson, *Claims to Fame: Celebrity in Contemporary America*. Berkeley and Los Angeles: University of California Press, 1994.

9. That these interests slowly become our realities is the argument of Theodor Adorno and Max Horkhiemer. In their discussion of cinema, for example, they argue, 'Real life is becoming indistinguishable from the movies. The sound film, far surpassing the theater of illusion, leaves no room for imagination or reflection on the part of the audience, who was unable to respond within the structure of the film, yet deviate from its precise detail without losing the thread of the story; hence the film forces its victims to equate it directly with reality.' Theodor W. Adorno and Max Horkhiemer, *Dialectic of Enlightenment*, trans. John Cumming. New York: Continuum, 1999, p. 126.

Part I

Creation

Chapter 1

Consuming Towards Exile

The end result of all consumption is excrement: we seek out our consumables, we consume, we digest and we defecate.

The Western experience is one of consumption. We consume food made by others, grown elsewhere, preserved artificially, hyper-nutritious or, more often, ultra-fatty. We consume clothing made by others, sewn by men and women over there – on the shelf, on the body, on the ground, on the way out. We consume images of us and others, sometimes naked, sometimes clothed. These images are used, deleted and eventually replaced. We consume music, downloaded, organized as lists, felt but not heard, heard with others watching, galvanized as digital bits, CD trays and booklets put aside, loaded into the trash, into the iPod.

All of these consumables start as splendour and end as less than that. They are the things we desperately want to have, at all costs, for no costs. As a kid, for me it was fast food. The greasy heights of emotion made possible by a White Castle hamburger spun my young eyes with delight. But when the consumption was over, the pleasure was gone – in one way and out another. This was all part of the rehearsed routine of fast food: love now, regret later. What is more American than this? To splurge then worry, to buy then think, to love the puppy and hate the dog.

We perform this process unwittingly. It only comes into focus when that which we consume sticks in our teeth, or fills up too much space, or haunts us while driving to work. Consider the consumption of Britney Spears. To begin, in what forms was she offered? As a child prodigy, a southern belle, an adolescent play thing, a body to be desired, a desire embodied, as a daughter, mother, divorcee, drug addict, as disabled, discouraged and down. Never as musician, never. And who did the offering? Lynne Spears, Disney, Sony BMG,

Eric Foster White, Max Martin, Rolling Stone, MTV, VH1, paparazzi, pornographers and, essentially, us. We pitched her, talked her up and down, loved her, hated her, praised the kid and demonized the older kid. She was given to us first in song, yet almost immediately we stopped listening and started watching. It was her smile, her hair, her breasts and buttocks, her legs, her feet. She was an image of a woman, and image only. This is how we wanted her, and this is what we consumed.

Britney Spears was consumed by children when she was still a child. And for a while, it was sweet to see a young girl in a Britney Halloween costume. Then the consuming changed. On 15 April 1999, Britney appeared on the cover of *Rolling Stone* for the first time. Her body became text, her eyes invited the gaze and her stomach made readers of all types look twice. And certainly this was by design, crafted to sell the body once safe in cotton sweaters on the Disney channel. Walt would not be happy. His disappointment would be a product of a shifting demographic. Men, young and old, gay and straight, became the key consumers of Britney the Body. Certainly, the girls and women were still there, they just had to shift over, make room.

Follow Britney's career post 15 April. First, see the girls buying her albums and bubble gum, listening to her music, looking for themselves, their stories, singing along without really understanding the words. Now see the men. See them watch her at the MTV Video Music Awards, stripping off a tear-away tuxedo, fondling a python and stumbling in a bikini too small for this 'not yet a woman' woman. See them watching videos of Britney in red and black leather, snarling the innocence away, showing just enough, shaking just enough; erotic and not, she played the Lolita and Lamb very well. See the men looking at thousands of images online, fake pornography with floating heads, stories upon stories about favourite positions, favourite foods, public displays of affection and ignorance. Britney split in two, image and body, soul and impression, good and bad.

The harder the consumer looked, the more sly she became, hiding a nipple, hiding behind the decency laws of television and the press. Her pregnant body, naked almost. A cultural hide and go seek. Then the infamous photo came, her in the backseat with Paris. When we saw her sex directly, it was over. Put more clearly, when we saw her naked, shaved crotch, the rules of the game had changed, rules that we all had agreed on. Britney was supposed to be perfect, distant yet close. We reached out to her in ways that we controlled. We were her, she was us, images and imaginations matched up perfectly.

But when we saw *it*, it wasn't perfect, airbrushed, smooth and clean. Instead it was human. It was real, complete with razor burn, flesh folds and use. No longer a collective vision of beauty, it was now hers; its particularity became crystal clear. We wanted to stay in Umberto Eco's hyperreality,[1] in the comforts of our own imaginations. The photograph ended it all. And then she shaved her head. Another blow to our lens.

And so like all things consumed, Britney was digested and eliminated. She made her way through our cultural gastrointestinal tract, broken down by the saliva of our desire, and excreted. Left to be what *Rolling Stone* called an American Tragedy, forgetting that they started the whole thing.[2]

And yet these metaphors of consumption, digestion and excretion let us off easy. The problem lies in the part called digestion. Consider the fact that most of us know very little about the art of digestion. It just happens. It's a process that starts up when it needs to, shuts down when it wants to, doing its job without much help. And this is exactly how we want and need it. It needs to be behind the wizard's curtain, otherwise it would make us sick. Oils and acids, churning our consumables into faeces. Not pretty, but necessary.

As such, our digestion of Britney was too natural, too easy, too unnoticed. Young Britney, Body Britney, Baby Britney, Broken Britney. We shifted and digested right through these transitions with a skipping pace. For a two-year period she was down for the count, having been excreted from our desires and imaginations. We had moved on, only to find ourselves missing her. Eventually, we would start eating again.

This collection of reflections about the life and art of Britney Spears offers a different lens to view this story – one of exile. The fall of Britney cannot be seen as a simple cultural inevitability. Too many artists and performers are brushed off by our Darwinian, nationalistic belief in the dismissal of the unworthy. The pitching of the Other. No, our response to (and creation of) Britney Spears was not this, but a violent form of cultural cleansing. She was dirty, and real, and repulsive. We made her this way by accepting years of objectification, by buying and selling her. To liken this to digestion is to remind ourselves that we were part of this. Unknowingly or not it was our energy that initiated the exile.

Britney is not innocent, but she is not alone in her story. It seems that we were there all along.

Notes

1. Semiotician Umberto Eco has written extensively on what he calls the 'hyperreal'. It is his conclusion that we have created for ourselves 'fortresses of solitude' in which we bathe ourselves in the pleasure of knowing nothing, in the splendour of the fantastic. The best examples of these fortresses include wax museums, Disney World and other tourist attractions including national parks, historical monuments and the like. Note his description of these fortresses: '... in America there are many Fortresses of Solitude, with their wax statues, their automata, their collections of inconsequential wonders. You have only to go beyond the Museum of Modern Arts and the art galleries, and you enter another universe, the preserve of the average family, the tourist, the politician.' Umberto Eco, *Travels in Hyperreality*. Orlando: Harcourt Brace & Company, 1986, pp. 5–6.
2. You can see the entire article online: Vanessa Grigoriadis, 'The Tragedy of Britney Spears', *Rolling Stone*, 21 February 2008, http://www.rollingstone.com/news/story/18310562/cover_story_the_tragedy_of_britney_spears.

Chapter 2

The Baptists

Why do we seek origins? This question tells us more about ourselves than the information we seek. At best, we seek origins to help make sense of a problem, to clarify a picture gone out of focus, to validate an opinion that needs justification. At worst, we seek the dirt of existence, the roots of some phenomenological system which fascinates us, a way to see through the darkly painted glass whose contents evade but also quench. We seek origins to keep from dealing with the reality of our situation, believing that if we know the beginning of the story its development and progression will somehow matter more or less. We hope that the dilemmas our reality makes us grapple with will dwindle a bit if we find their origins. Why did the planes hit the towers? Why did Chapman shoot Lennon in front of The Dakota? Why did God let disability embrace my kid? Why am I fat? Questions that keep us from letting the thing settle in, from being real. Anything to keep busy, to keep talking. We love dialogue, even the word (di-a-log) makes us sound sophisticated.

The only thing that remains sophisticated, however, is our evasion of realness. All too often, we seek origins to keep from doing the real work of being present. However, we must acknowledge the possibility that presentness guides our search for origins, that our vision of the current drives to its bias, a lens that admits its own construction. And so we seek origins with our heads up, with our eyes open. Our story of Britney Spears, too, starts with our knowledge of her contemporary existence. We know she has recently been in a psych ward, exploring explanations, reading up on herself, digesting our digestion, sifting through our excrement. Currently she is being babysat while she babysits, ready to ride the wave of her next 'comeback'. The new record, *Circus*, is selling well, concerts are being sold out again.

When I look up McComb, Mississippi on Wikipedia I learn three facts: it was named after a Colonel Henry McComb, former head of the Great Northern Railroad; it was the cradle of the Civil Rights Movement, harbouring the first action of the Student Nonviolent Coordinating Committee; it is near the swamp that saw the end of Ronnie Van Zant and Steve Gaines of Lynyrd Skynyrd. Trains, pains and planes. Garrison Keillor might say, 'Well, it was a town like most towns', and then exhale loudly. As of 2000, about 14,000 called it home, and a bunch of others remembered it as such. Britney Jean Spears, born there on 2 December 1981, is among them.

Her parents, the well-known Lynn and lesser-known James (or Jamie), were respectively a teacher and a building contractor. Humble yet pretty, quiet yet stern. You have to wonder if they knew their baby would be special, be someone others looked up to, someone to love. Yes, all parents think this, but books, newspapers and magazines all tell us that the Spears *knew* this. They knew that little Britney would be, if it took all they had, someone special. They moved the family to Kentwood, Mississippi, for work and new linoleum.

Siblings were born, diapers were changed, groceries were bagged up and the family went on.

Like Elvis, Aretha, Tina and all other musical artists who matter the most, Britney sang in the church choir as a child. Great, creaky, Baptist hymns that made bodies sway, made children seek their origins. Margo Jefferson, in her revealing book *On Michael Jackson*, alludes to the words to this Baptist hymn which no doubt Britney heard as well:

> Little lamb, who made thee?
> Dost thou know who made thee,
> Gave thee life, and bade thee feed
> By the stream and o'er the mead;
> Gave thee clothing of delight,
> Softest clothing, woolly, bright;
> Gave thee such a tender voice,
> Making all the vales rejoice?
> Little lamb, who made thee?
> Dost thou know who made thee?[1]

Such questions lingered on the faith of the Baptist brethren and their lambs, theological inquiries made sweet in songs. The answer to this spiritual riddle, of course, is God, the I Am, the present-through-Jesus-Christ-Creator. And yet the Spears shared the creation work with God, and eventually so did we.[2]

The Baptist side of Britney secured some things for her: she was born into sin, saved through baptismal immersion, bought by the death of Jesus, made new through the Holy Spirit and chastened to an evangelical, gospel-filled existence. She was an image bearer of God, emblazed by the mark of the true covenant. Of course, a child struggles to know what any of this means, as do many adults, but certainly on both they have at least a cumulative effect. She knew, again, that she was special, that she belonged to something bigger, something much larger than herself.

In some ways, this is a given, a particularity that is not very particular at all. Most of us grow up in homes where faith, of some kind, is a member of the family. Which means that along with being a member of a biological and genetic grouping known as our 'family', we are also part of an invisible collective, a larger family of strangers. A community of saints, angels, prophets and ministers. Britney began as a member of a spiritual culture, one which cradled her, crafted her and called her out. And it is this last action, this calling out, that seems so relevant now. As a Southern Baptist, young Britney would have been called to consider the world in a very specific way – in particular, she would have be asked to see the outside world as something which needed her – a world that needed Jesus to be seen through her.

She began her life with a mission, one which asked her to live for others. Even further, a mission which asked her to live for those who were perceived as needing her and the gospel message – to testify to this Other as a messenger of the good news, as a portal through which God's love could be seen. She would be a lens for those in need, a way for them to see clearer the better ways of life. At home she could still play with dolls, do her make-up like mommy, make up songs. But on Sunday morning, singing with the choir, she was on. The spotlight of the holy spirit itself illuminated this blonde angel in a way that she must have developed a feeling for. How could she not have? Because along with serving God through the ministry of music, Britney was also learning to love the attention that comes to those who serve the Lord. A sort of righteous attention on one level, but a very cultural attention on another.

Such a beginning. A self-understanding of yourself as being made by God, in His image, in his everlasting arms. Such lessons lead to confidence – a known self is a powerful self. Brought further, this identity attaches you to a cultural and cosmic community, a congregation and the Family of God. The sense of belonging times two. A lifescape with an intended audience, a constant performance of being, proving that you are God's by bringing Him to all those around you, both saved and unsaved, alive or dead. A stage has been set for you before you are aware of what that means. And your goals are predestined, you follow a road well travelled, yet never touched by feet like yours. A quest to be among others as a sign of something good, as something to be treasured, as something to be desired. Amen, halleluiah.

As a guide for life and a predicted trajectory, the teachings of the Southern Baptists launched Britney into a psychology well suited for performance. Not only did it prepare her to perform, it provided a space for her to act and justified her desire for the spotlight.

And it also gave her an ideology to react to. No worldview makes sense until it is smashed against the wall, worked on, challenged to stand next to another. The same vision of life that originally gave Britney a song, gave her a way out as well. A sort of reverse-ideology, a manner of experiences always seen best through its backdrop, a career with a much needed context: impurity looks good when set against an original purity; the body as desired object shines in the context of the body as a temple; the tongue of the vixen versus the tongues of Babel; the breasts of high school fun in front of the breastplate of righteousness; fierce independence overshadows interdependence; profanity explained through praise; sacrifice in light of, holy sacrifice.

So the psychology of faith makes itself known in Britney in the same way any ideology would – as anchor and reverberation. Early interviews, overexposed by the secular media and questioned by religious media, see Britney holding on to spiritual tenets from her childhood faith: she sings because she loves; she sings for God; she keeps her virginity for the right man. These are anchors of action. At the same time, she enacts a sort of call and response ritual, a reactionary and ironic performance. She sings because she loves us, but also in order for us to love her; she sings for God, but also for heaps and heaps of money; she waits for the right man yet flaunts for all, wearing a Catholic schoolgirl outfit.

On one level these dichotomies and ironies must be (and have been) seen as promotional. P.T. Barnum taught us well the lessons of contrast. It is one thing to see a bearded lady, but it is completely other to see her in a wedding dress. Fat men boggle the brain of the spectator, but even more so when placed naked on a couch. The aesthetics of spectacle have always been invested in exploiting context as much as content; to know the true attraction is to know how grandly it compares to its surroundings.[3] Add sexuality to this formula and, bingo! the bank is yours. A sexy girl contextualized by her own religious context – that is a promotion of the century. Something forbidden made available and affordable, something holy made hot, something good made bad.

And yet, at another level, one led by psychology, we might come to see these paradoxical predicaments of Britney's faith and performance as being the first step towards an unavoidable pathology. A condition in which her own origins get murky as her present and future experiences take over. A predicament that asks her to defend something personal in relationship to something very public. And isn't this the American pathology made blaringly clear via the cultural stage? All individuals feeding from the trough of individualism must suffer this, or celebrate this lot – that our insides can be different from our outsides. That we can and must decide, based on political, economic and social factors, what we want others to know of us. We, and only we, can decide which face to show and why.

Faith, perhaps, is the clearest illustration of this tricky business of show and tell. Philosopher and cultural critic James Olthuis maps out this terrain in terms of worldviews, which he defines as the answers we give to important questions about our identity (who am I?), our earthly experience (why am I here?) and our transcendental hopes (is there a God, who is He/She?).[4] The answers we give to these questions are on one hand very personal, and by extension, private. However, in order to fit in with others like us, which is to say live meaningfully, we must let some of these answers out. We must take the risk of making them public. Those of us who live in the Western world, specifically in the United States, have really messed this up. We have made the natural process of communicating faith and belief into something unnatural. What was once sharing in order to live communally is now admitting in order to justify or sanctify. Our anchors, as a consequence, become our ballast – things which are perceived as keeping us down.

Certainly, the hyper-public nature of Britney Spears the performer forced Britney the Baptist to deal with these issues head on, in the cultural spotlight, way too early in her life. How many seventeen-year-old girls are asked, on *60 Minutes*, to defend a worldview? Then again, how many seventeen year olds get to ask their friends, 'What should I wear when all the world is watching?' I ask this to remind us that Britney, or her management, was actively involved in the predicament currently under our surveillance. In the end, while we developed the picture, she offered its negative.

So, what of origins, hers and ours? Faith provided Britney with an introductory lens of the world, one in which she saw herself as God's, and consequently, the world's. It gave her membership in a community of saints, a sense of being needed, the mandatory feeling (for those destined to live public lives) of purpose. In addition, it gave her something to react to, something to rebel against, something to compare her performing self to. On the surface at least, it seems to have inspired, promoted, challenged and alienated her. A multifaceted halo. For us, the consumer, it offered a way inside. A way to claim ownership. A way to make her American, a saint and a sinner. In a very real way, the cultural conversations about Britney's journey of faith, which would eventually make stops at the Kabala and Hinduism, some vague form of humanism and eventually return to a faith which involves a God known by all middle-class Americans, were our way of making her ours. She was a product of our history, of our baggage, of our struggles. And then it sinks in – she is our origin.

Notes

1. Margot Jefferson, *On Michael Jackson*. New York: Vintage Books, 2007, p. 27. I was reading Jefferson's book while putting together the notes for this manuscript and it should be obvious throughout that I was inspired by her study. So much of what she argues about Michael Jackson has a direct connection with my own thoughts about Britney Spears, including particular interests in religion, sexuality and celebrity spectacle.
2. There are many resources available regarding the tenants of Baptist theology. Please see the following for a brief introduction: R. Stanton Norman, *The Baptist Way: Distinctives of a Baptist Church*. Nashville: Broadman & Holman Publishers, 2005; Fischer Humphreys, *The Way We Were: How Southern Baptist Theology Has Changed and What it Means to Us All*. Macon: Smyth & Helwys Publishing Inc., 2002.
3. For an introduction to the literature on freaks see: Robert Bogdan, *Freak Show: Presenting Human Oddities for Amusement and Profit*. Chicago and London: The University of Chicago Press, 1990; Rosemarie Garland Thomson, *Extraordinary Bodies: Figuring Physical Disability in American Culture and Literature*. New York: Columbia University Press, 1997 and Garland Thomson, ed., *Freakery: Cultural Spectacles of the Extraordinary Body*. New York: New York University Press, 1996; Marlena Tromp, ed., *Victorian Freaks*. Columbus: The Ohio State University Press, 2008. You will see in these works that there is no consensus about the cultural value of presenting people with disabilities as freaks. For example, Robert Bogdan argues convincingly that the freak of the nineteenth century should be seen as an intelligent, resourceful entrepreneur using his or her body as a means of capital and social identity. On the contrary, Garland Thomson views the practice of freak exhibition as a point of historical oppression for people with disabilities.
4. James Olthuis, 'On Worldviews'. In Paul Marshall, Sander Griffioen and Richard Mouw, eds, *Stained Glass: Worldviews and Social Science*. Lanham: University Press of America, 1989, pp. 26–40.

Chapter 3

The South

When one's character begins to fall under suspicion and disfavor, how swift, then, is the work of disintegration and destruction.

Mark Twain[1]

The South is a complicated matrix of ideas, stereotypes, histories and really good-tasting food. So complicated is this collection of impressions that beyond geographical specificity, we who have not called Dixie home cannot, in any precise way, claim to really know The South. We know *of* The South. We know of the southern accent, of the drawl that indicates more than it actually implicates; we know of the racism, pictured and filmed during those hot summer days of the 1860s and 1960s; we know those signs and symbols of The South hopping and hicking their ways through Bugs Bunny cartoons, *Ma and Pa Kettle* cinema shows and *Saturday Night Live* skits. The South that most know is actually not The South at all. Instead, like most cultural knowledge, our concepts of The South come on the back of an awkward anthropology, one justified and perpetuated by distant observation. We deny Bronislaw Malinowski and his participant observation, preferring instead to 'participate' from our set of guide books and travelogues.[2] We like our rendering of The South too much to surrender it to anything authentic.

Because we craft The South from nowhere, we are consequently able to employ The South. It is a non-place.[3] As an entity brought to the surface primarily by connotation and context, The South is marked as an adjective waiting to happen; if we like the music of Stephen Foster we invoke The South as the quaint centrifuge hurling 'Oh, Susannah!' from the picnic voices; when we turn away from lynching pictures, we blame The South and its grip on those folks 'picnicking' their way to hell. In other words, rather than know The South, we actually use it. We use it when we vote, when we sing and dance, when we eat, drink and play, when we conjure up America in classrooms, when we want to feel sad and mournful, and when we want to feel good about where we are today.

That Britney Spears is from The South, then, can paradoxically mean so much and so little. Knowing her southern roots can become a sort of Janus-faced beast of burden, a reason to look forward or a reason to look back. Her southerness is a heritage which we can use to hurt or heal the consumed and exiled body of Britney, just as long as our looking remains consistent with our seeing – The South can only be used in the analysis of Ms Spears if it is allowed to actually be The South of our minds, good and bad. Cotton is soft, but only after it makes its picker's fingers bleed.

The South we most easily employ is the one that trivializes, the one that tears down those who come from a place where we assume education means very little, where mud puddles stain the farm that is barely feeding the family, where politics are painted red and hoods are white. This is The South of the ignorant, conjured by ignorance. And it is an ignorance that allows offensive questions to fly from our lips – how can they be so racist, how can they live like that, how come they talk like that, how come they are not like us? The South of the ignorant brands southerners the bearers of bad luck history, as inheritors of an ideology beyond their own understanding. In other words, Britney might know where she comes from, but she is too ignorant to understand what that origination actually means.

But actually, her ignorance doesn't matter because we know what it means.

'We, the consumer, do solemnly swear, with our God as our witness, to know Britney the southerner as a bona fide piece of lily white trash. This truth we hold to be self-evident as we watch her start smokin' in paparazzi pictures, crackin' open Budweisers yellin' "yee haw!" from her Jeep, wearin' Daisy Dukes to the beach, spittin' and cussin' in public, holdin' hands with the skuzzy fellar from her video, eatin' way too much chicken for one gal, mixin' with the wrong posse. Damn, ya'll, what she thinkin'?'

One answer: nothing at all. A more interesting answer is that she was thinking about moving on.

When we spotted 'white trash' Britney for the first time, it was kind of exciting. Something new for us to try on, like a May bathing suite. As more of The South seeped from the historical pores of Britney Jean, however, this newness quickly got old. We began to recognize it as that old southern shtick. The modern of Britney gave way to the antique of The South. And really, we didn't like it. The accent was cute, a tidbit of southern belle that sexualized her in a way that we learned from Dolly Parton. Attached to that there was a sort of innocence, again sexualized, that suited the blonde hair and smile. In other words, we liked The South when it peeked its head up now and then. But all the time, swinging and snarling, was just too much. In Britney Jean we saw the buck-toothed, butt-cracked, farmer-tanned idiot who brewed moonshine on the weekends. She became the redneck at the wedding, dancing too crazy to Alabama records, spitting chew behind the church. She became the lousy mom without a car seat, slapping on lipstick too red. In short, for the folks who knew the MTV Britney,

Ms Britney Jean of The South was the alien, migrant worker who stained impressions and left them feeling dirty and wrong. More succinctly, southern Britney was not their Britney. She had shed the 'be-new, buy-me-as-something-new' by-product body of the mass culture game, and dived back into the old ways of her cradle.

This dive could have marked a real turning point for Britney. I have always thought that The South could have actually saved her from the absurdity that had, by 2003, become her life of gesture. Feel The South, Ms Spears. Arthur G. Pettit, one of many biographers of Samuel Clemens, reminds his readers that The South has been penned many, many ways – as burden, as curse, as enigma, as irony, riddle and tragedy.[4] And while a surface glance at the list may provoke a cringe of northern pride, a deeper, honest glance might just as well produce knowledge and insight. Read the list like a Twain story – salty and a bit dark on the outside, but tender and quite splendid on the inside. A punch that ends with an embrace.

So, feel The South, Ms Spears. Rather than wear it, feel it. Not in a touchy *feely* way, but feel it in a bone-splitting, vision-enhancing, spit-tasting way. Too much has been asked of Britney for me to make such a request, but times are desperate. She's too young to get it? No, not really. We all understand space, time and place at a very young age, we just can't articulate it.[5] Who am I to offer articulation of The South? A white guy from the Midwest fumbling through impressions and expectations, dabbling in cultural tourism, and feasting on the spectacle of cultural knowledge? – but also attempting to break my own bones here, alter my own visions, swallow a new spit.

So, Ms Spears, let's you and me feel The South: pitch the caricatures and really try to understand the richness and heritage of the place, the pain and joy of its time, and the intimate contours of its space. In other words, let's allow The South to do what it has apparently never done for you, for me, for the MTV crowd, for the paparazzi, for your countless connoisseurs, for most folks – let's allow The South to feel us. Let it wander in our imagination by its own volition, crawl freely in our minds without us leading the way. All history is interpretation, yet it shouldn't just be our interpretation, but that of others, trusted others, black and white, male and female, rich and poor others. This is not simply a call for authenticity, like there exists just around the corner some *authentic* southerness. Indeed, it is a call to strike down the beast of authenticity! And on our way home from the hunt, we need to pick up little pieces of The South, let them pick us up, carry us for a while, so that when we return we are rested, and ready, to let the experience of this place be what it is.

I wonder if Flannery O'Connor's sketches and carvings of southern life might help us.[6] As a tour guide for the uninformed she might very well be a dangerous choice, but really all tour guides are risky at this level. All of the many folks we might pick here have that pesky human quality of subjectivity and bias. And yet, this personified Southerness is exactly what we need. We need to take a grand step away from the objectification of objective renditions of The South, the false negatives that we have developed over the years. Instead of enrolling our attitudes in sessions of ignorant fact-bending it will serve us well to see Britney's Southern identity as being something lived and felt in a way that was odd thanks only to the fact that it was done so on a cultural stage.

O'Connor's southerness was deeply embedded, and it remained so until she died of lupus in August of 1964. Her South, for it was distinctly hers, existed and took shape somewhere between the auspicious and the grotesque. The characters of her stories mark a path for her readers that has always reminded me of a tree-lined, gravel road from my childhood summer home. During the hot hours of daylight from an August sun, the big Michigan pine trees offered shelter, safety, cool air. But at night, when the moon took over the sun's place, things changed. The road took on a different character. Those trees which had guarded me now haunted me. They became creatures, and not good ones. The road which was smooth and passable became bumpy, unsure and wrong. Such are the stories of Flannery O'Connor.

That road always reminded me of the grandmother in her story about the misfit.[7] Is the grandma The South? Is the grandma, this awkward and tragic woman, somehow a snapshot of southern life? Ambitious, yet always cranky, in the light of the summer morning, turning a little unsure of herself as the sun set on the hot afternoon day with the family in the car. Full of life, and in an instant full of death. The audacity of family life slapped down by the vital mess of the grotesque. Flannery O'Connor gave us a glimpse of what The South meant to her in this character, in all of her characters. She offered, in other words, a representation of The South that was deeply rooted in her own living, in her own bones.

I don't actually think that O'Connor can give us a true sense of what it means to be southern. Indeed, such an offering is unavailable. However, her stories give us a vision of The South that is embedded, again, within something well-rooted in her soul. We never got this from Britney. We never allowed her to give that to us. Indeed, none of her art was ever rooted below the Dixie line. It was all Los Angeles, California, slapped together with glam and glitz, always something new, overdone. What Flannery O'Connor had the opportunity to do in her short stories was to slow down. To make us slow down. We paid the dollar, we followed her, and she gave us a report on what southern living meant to her.

The grandmother in her story might actually be us. We take a trip into The South just like she took a trip that day. Our trip may not end like hers, but in many ways we are the awkward backseat passenger. In fact most of us are passengers when it comes to The South. We take our trips, we talk about what we saw, we represent what we saw to those who have not been there with us.

The Band did this, and oh, how sweet and gritty was their report. Listen to their accounts of The South from 1968 and 1969. For me, The South that The Band found was most clearly felt in the vocal cords of Levon Helm and through the fierce and frenetic fingers of Garth Hudson. Listen to the strained tones as Helm sings from *The Band*, an obvious yet so important example:

> Like my father before me, I will work the land,
> Like my brother above me, who took a rebel stand.
> He was just eighteen, proud and brave, But a Yankee laid him in his grave,
> I swear by the mud below my feet,
> You can't raise a Caine back up when he's in defeat.

When this song was recorded, Helm was the only member of the ensemble actually from the South, born in Elaine, Arkansas in 1940. The other guys were from Canada. This is significant for two reasons. First, who else but a blood born southerner could sing these words, could swim atop the social and political context of a refrain so steeped with time and space? And second, that Helm was the only member from the South speaks volumes about the potential for transference of regional value. It can be done without too much artifice, without so much spectacle, without an abundance of stereotypes. Members of The Band got it without flaunting it.[8] They borrowed but gave back. Britney either forgot to do this, or, more realistically, wasn't allowed to. Her South was worn like LA leather, sleeked up and sparkly. It was, put another way, just another photo op.

Yet I am not sure that it could have been any other way. Britney has never been, nor will she ever be, something grounded – the pop culture machine makes certain of that. To be grounded is to be distinct, to be marginalized, to be zoned off. Such a state lessens marketability. The Band knew this. And I think we can say that Flannery O'Connor knew it as well.

And so while Ms Spears from The South appeared for us to chew on for a while, she could not remain. Her handlers would not have that, nor would we. Not only because we stereotype The South, not because we misunderstand our history, that's not why this southern suspicion began and ended. Instead, it was because we saw the monster take refuge. We heard the machine sputter a bit, as if it might slow down. That Britney might find some foothold, some stability, in a place that so few of her fans could relate to, was the real scandal. We loathed The South of Spears because it marked the possibility of an end. And no place or thing was going to take that job away from us.

The paradox of all of this, of course, is that while The South can be seen as a non-place it can also be seen as an anchor. This is so true when we look at it through the lens of Britney Spears. It comes down to what we really need The South to be, us and Britney. And the problem is, our answers to this question are always convoluted, mixed up by our own emotions, needs, and desires. Britney needed The South to be her home, to be her anchor, to be a place in which she could secure a position that was away from the machine. Instead, never wanting her to stop, we could never let the South be that for her. We needed it to be a playground, a place where we can have fun with her yet somehow always without her. An amusement park of spectacles and stereotypes, where we run the rides, and run them a little too fast, a little too chaotically, for our one and only passenger.

Notes

1. Quoted in Clara Clemens, *My Father Mark Twain*. New York: Harpers, 1931, p. 86.
2. Bronislaw Malinowski revolutionized the practice of ethnography by demonstrating a method of social inquiry called 'participant observation' in which the ethnographer gathered 'data' about a people group not by simply observing them from a distance, but by living with them for an extended period of time. For an accessible introduction to his work see Bronislaw Malinowski, Michael W. Young, ed., *The Ethnography of Malinowski: The Trobriand Islands 1915–18*. London: Routledge & Kegan Paul Ltd, 1979.
3. Anthropologist Marc Augé defines his precarious term 'non-places' in the following manner: 'If a place can be defined as relational, historical, and concerned with identity, then a space which cannot be defined as relational, or historical, or concerned with identity will be a non-place. The hypothesis advanced here is that supermodernity produces non-places, meaning spaces which are not themselves anthropoligical places and which, unlike Baudelairean modernity, do not integrate the earlier places: instead these are listed, classified, promoted to the status of "places of memory", and assigned to a circumscribed and specific position.' Marc Augé, *Non-places: An Introduction to an Anthropology of Supermodernity*. London: Verso Press, 1995, p. 78.
4. Arthur G. Pettit, *Mark Twain and the South*. Lexington: University of Kentucky Press, 1974, pp. 5–6.
5. Author and cultural critic bell hooks has written beautifully on the idea of place, location, and longing. Note how she defines place as much more than geography: 'I need to live where I can walk. I need to be able to walk to work, to the store, to a place where I can sit and drink tea and fellowship. Walking, I will establish my presence, as one who is claiming the Earth, creating a sense of belonging, a culture of place.' Certainly, as I am arguing in this book, Britney Spears would have benefited a great deal from this type of understanding of place, more specifically of The South. See bell hooks, *Belonging: A Culture of Place*. New York: Routledge, 2009, p. 2.
6. My thoughts on Flannery O'Connor are influenced greatly by theologian and cultural critic David Dark. For his analysis please see David Dark, *Everyday Apocalypse: The Sacred Revealed in Radiohead, The Simpsons and Other Pop Culture Icons*. Grand Rapids: Brazos Press, 2002, pp. 27–41.
7. The full story about the grandmother in the backseat can be found in O'Connor's story 'A Good Man is Hard to Find'. In Flannery O'Connor, *A Good Man is Hard to Find*. New Brunswick: Rutgers, 1993, pp. 31–54.
8. The most eloquent analysis of The Band can be found in Grail Marcus, *Mystery Train: Images of America in Rock 'n' Roll Music*. 4th ed. New York: Plume, 1997, pp. 39–64.

Chapter 4

The Family

Families are difficult. I love my family, yet they make me have eyeball-pinching headaches. I love my family, yet they do frustrate me beyond belief, like a dog that won't stop biting at a shoestring. I also love my family because they make me who I am, because when I look at them I can see the beginnings of me. I love my family like I love an old shirt; it feels good to have it on, to have them on. The other day, my son, eighteen months old, decided to put his baby monitor in the toilet. Was I angry? Yes. But I also couldn't stop laughing. Neither could he.

But enough about me. And really, enough about you and your family. This is not about us – it's about her. This is about her family problems, her family drama, her family predicament. Of course, we've convinced ourselves that because of some unspoken set of rules, the Spears family is not really a family at all – they don't send Christmas cards, they don't share family dinners together, they don't do family like we do. Instead, they are members of a drama troupe, a collective of actors and players meant to entertain, horrify and feed a hungry audience. But they do not provide us with the fake family window that the Brady's or Partridges once did. Their family life does not provide a mirror through which we are able to reflect on our own relationships with mom, dad, brother and sister. They are a narrative, a collection of artificial vignettes, and as such, we know their beginnings, their tragic middle, and we think we know the ending. Our families are living, breathing narratives; the Spears are dormant. We buy their family albums at the checkout line in grocery stores, we see their family movies on late-night television. They are quiescent because they are entertainment.

So much has been said about the Spears family. Take a few steps back from the television and the magazine and catch the peculiar pop-culture paradox – the reality that we have said so much, and yet so very little. Again, this is not a family we are talking about. These are cardboard cutouts of people. And so while we talk, and talk, about what they have done wrong, about how backwards they are, about how we would never do what they have done, we are really saying nothing at all about that which is real. We have been armchair anthropologists speaking without conviction, articulating without consequence, marking without a map. If we are to speak about her family, and actually hear ourselves, our work has yet to be done. Understanding that Britney comes from a family is to understand that Britney is more than the exiled, the lost, the lonely. She is the offspring of something much larger than her. She is a by-product of something more than popular culture: she is a substance brought into this world, painfully, by a woman who we have villainized; she is the daughter of a silent man; she is the sister to a troubled girl and a brother that tries to keep his distance. In short, she is an honest to God family member whether we want to admit it or not.

Last commencement, I met one of my favourite student's parents. They were from North Carolina, and the father had worked with the Spears family when Disney made them famous for the first time. We were having one of those awkward, yet wonderful conversations. They don't know me, I don't know them, but we are brought together by our one point of interection, my student, their kid. When I mentioned that I was writing this book, the father said, 'Oh really?' in a way that suggested he had more to say. So naturally I dug a bit.

'Yes, it has been a very interesting project.'

(He bit.)

'Yes, I imagine it would be.' He smiles.

I am ready for the dirt.

'I'm in show business, did my kid tell you that?'

(He had.)

'I met the Spears family and, well … I guess it would have been 1992. They were just getting hooked up on the Disney Channel. Crazy family. Absolutely crazy.'

And with that, we laughed a bit. While he moved down to meet some of my colleagues, I quickly jotted down a note.

Investigative, celebrity journalism is perhaps the most rotten part of our collective behaviour and yet it is so irresistible, to the point of seeming necessary. We purge in front of televisions, as the 'reporters' perch on trees, roofs and our attention. They tell us everything we want to know while at the same time absolutely nothing is given to us. Fancy packages with nothing inside. Well, there is something inside, but nothing we would like to take home to mom.

Celebrity journalism is really an oxymoron, a funny way of saying that we need to know more about the people we already know more about. It's a conundrum that most don't really think about. As always, these cultural procedures say more about us than the people they directly concern. But again, that's an old argument, one which, deep down, we already know.

But, quickly for those who have not tuned in – celebrity journalism is not journalism at all. Celebrity journalism is a mirror through which we should be able to see our own pain, dissatisfaction and envy. Celebrity journalism is a trough from which we feed mindlessly. Celebrity journalism acts like a dagger, a splintery tool that scars us as well as them. Celebrity journalism is fun, but only in the way eating too many candy bars is fun – it tastes so good now, but punishes us later. In this way, eating celebrities is a sort of unconscious cannibalism. Chewy, chewy souls, chewy, chewy bodies, chewy, chewy people.

And so the note I wrote down after speaking with the dad from North Carolina read something like this: where do we get our knowledge of Britney Spears' family, and why do we care so much about them?

Remove the burden of proof, in all its impossible forms, and you will begin to see an answer to the first question. Celebrity knowledge of any kind is always based in a sort of discourse, a sort of give and take (more like take and give). In other words, there is no standardization by which we might say, without question, that we *know* the celebrities we follow. Instead, what we really know is how people talk about them. What we really know is based in a sort of conversational reality. Some reporter says that Britney's mom and her have a falling out, that money-talk was involved and that they are not on speaking terms. This reporter is actually not a reporter at all. Instead, she acts as a sort of ignorant interlocutor, a craftsperson whose art is paraphrasing and partiality.

Indeed she is an artist, one that we have commissioned again and again. And if we could see her as an artist this game would be much more interesting. Consider what would happen if we allowed celebrity journalism to be a sort of art form. On what criteria would we value the merits of this art? Or, perhaps the better question would be, what wouldn't we value this art by? If we carry with us the criteria of traditional art criticism we would quickly learn that truthfulness would not be that helpful in our analysis.

But what do we mean by 'truthfulness'? And further, what do we mean by 'art'? These are loaded words. Loaded by us, by *them*, by a whole community of folks who enter this discussion from many angles.

Picture in your mind the works of Jackson Pollock, Claude Monet, Tom Thompson, Frida Kahlo, or any other painter that makes sense to you. As you look at the shapes, strokes and sensibilities of these works, ask yourself how truth might play a part in valuing these paintings? Has the artist played with truth, replicated truth, or completely disregarded it? Push further, what do we mean by truth within the context of visual art? If we speak of Truth, with a capital T, then we are speaking of Universal Truth. This is the kind of truth that is just out of our reach, tempting us with stories and words but never embracing us, or giving us comfort. We can speak of multiple truths, those things that resonate with experience. Either way, when we think of truth and art we are often playing fast with our words. What are we talking about? Is it the modernist sense of truth, a privileged rationality and logic? Is it the postmodern truth, a splendid splintering of voice, consciousness and opinion? Going back even further, is it a romantic truth? Does it find its origin in those essential places of our souls?

Within these sets of questions, Truth doesn't get us very far in our evaluation of any text, let alone a person. Put more plainly, truth makes the whole endeavour of understanding anything a little bit messy. And it is this messiness that brings us back to our interlocutor artist, the celebrity journalists. Truth, with a capital T, makes no sense in terms of this art form and our understanding of it. Yet truth, or its impression, seems to be the very thing we value when we watch or read stories about Britney Spears in the media. The words uttered by our celebrity journalists are beads of condensation from Marshall McLuhan's cool medium – they are not truth, but portals of truth.[1] It takes us, and our action, to validate them as truth for us. And this personalized truth, this carving that we all do, reminds us again that we are co-conspirators. That we take an active role in the art form of crafting celebrity life.

This shared scheme of truth-making in popular culture experience is exactly what John Fiske meant when he said that we are enablers of our own pleasure when it comes to television and popular media.[2] Take note of the contours of this argument, let them sink in. It is too simple to believe that television, or any other popular media, has its way with us. That we are sponges, merely sucking in the mantras of electronic media, is a lazy lament. Celebrity journalism offers us Britney Spears and her family, but really that's where they stop. It's our work, our digestion, that places meaning on this form of communication. We take pleasure in working on what they give us – we love to spill out the message given to us, articulate it with friends, pick at it in our own way.

So when we speak of truth or art in the context of celebrity journalism and its report on the Britney Spears dilemma, we are really speaking of our own actions. We are the artists, we are the crafters of truth. And what is so astounding is that we do this unconsciously, and that we do it so well. Pick a medium of art as a metaphor, and follow it through. We are the sculptors cutting away at our object, moulding it into our shapes, feeling it with our fingers. We are the painters, manipulating our brushes on oils and canvas. We are the architects who meld materials together in order to construct a space. These art forms are both creative and destructive. We build up and break down material in order to claim a sort of truth, an image which represents all that we desire and love and need. In our discussions of the Spears family, aren't we doing the same thing? They are the material and we are the hands that shape it, mould it, destroy it, create it.

Where do we get our information about the Spears family? From us. From our work.

And as we let this answer settle in we stumble across the answer for our second question – why do we care so much about them? We care, with intensity, because they are ours.They are ours in the many senses of the word. At the most base level, they are ours because we have made them, we have crafted them, we are their creators. We should be puzzled at this point because this characteristic of them is rarely evident. Notice how this plays out when Britney thanks her fans at an awards show. 'Thank you for making me who I am!' How odd. But not in the way that we think. If we follow one line of thinking, we might say that indeed we have been responsible for making her who she is, both positive and negative. Follow another train of thought, the one being cultivated here, and in fact we might see that it is absurd for Britney Spears to allow herself to be created by people she does not know. She left that for the people she did know. But looking at it from our vantage point, even the unconscious one, we did actually make her. By buying albums, posters, CDs, concert tickets, tabloid journalism, Internet postings, and the like, we made her. She is ours. Fans of Britney know this in their hearts while critics of Ms Spears and her family tend to ignore it. If they did acknowledge it they would be out of work.

Yet ownership goes so much further in the case of Britney Spears and her family. Our creation of the Spears family is tied to something deeply American. The project, for lack of a better term, is one of experiential nationalism. To know what it means to be an American can only be felt through experience. Americanism is not something you get from reading a book, seeing a play or listening to a marching band. Rather, it is something you must taste and craft with your own senses. Pushing further, to know your experience of Americanism is to place you in competition with others. A pride, a nationalism, that can only be defended by you. But what makes this so odd is that while you are asking someone to feel what you feel, you are simultaneously telling them that they will never be able to do so. Thus is the case in our understanding of the Spears family. For even though they have been made to represent family darkness, illegitimacy, manipulation and greed, they are also American in a very particular fashion. They started from nothing. They captured the mythology of the age. Their celebrity was essential, something innate. They could only do what they have done in America.

On a website you can see the actual signature of Britney's great-grandfather, June Becker Spears, given at Ellis Island in the 1920s. Consequently, her American roots are well known, even digitally represented for us to contemplate. From these beginnings follow the American family. A quiet, hard-working father. A beautiful mother, blonde and at home taking care of the children. An older son who was the star of the football team, a middle daughter who could sing like an angel, and a younger daughter who could follow in her footsteps, loving grandparents, all of who played a role in the lives of the children. Southern barbecues, Sunday mornings at church. Then that middle child gains celebrity on a talent show, walks into Walt Disney World and takes over, becomes famous. The parents get divorced, the mother goes a little wacky, the younger daughter gets pregnant. All of the markings are there. They are us, the American family. And if we say this, then we must admit that their tragedy is ours as well. But isn't that American? To fess up to our infidelities, to take ownership of where we have gone wrong? Not really. Instead, we try to explain ourselves. Yes we did that, but here is why. And in the end, we hope that people forget what we actually did. We hope that they are caught up in our story, in our narrative.

Because in the end, and this should sound very familiar, the Spears family joined the list of things American which are also dispensable. Resources, family farms, waste, the working poor, the disabled, animals, elections – all of these things can easily be swept under the carpet of looking good. Britney and her family join this list because of us. They are American in every sense of the word, bad or good.

Finally, and this is where the bite really comes, they are ours because we would not like it any other way. We enjoy the Spears family, and our construction of it, because when the TV is turned off, the magazine is put away and the Internet is slowed to a low hum, and our smart phones are charging, we need them to be who they are. We need them to be the spectacle that we have made them. Guy DeBord explains this well when he says that spectacle is our environment, that we are a society of spectacle.[3] In other words, the Spears family in all its spectacle is really not an entity of its own but rather an atmosphere. It is the air that we breathe, the arena in which we work and play, the stuff that makes 'out there' happen. Thus, the particular of the Spears family becomes particle. Place this into a philosophical construct for a minute. Ask this question: what happens when people, living beings, become the air we breathe? What happens when the essential unit of a family becomes a mood, or a situation to react to? Pushing further, following hard ideas that we have tried to discuss above, what happens when this atmosphere is self-created? What happens when our environment becomes completely person made? When all that is natural is pushed aside, torn down, replaced?

The answer is actually quite simple: obliteration, in its most violent form.

Notes

1. McLuhan famously discussed the difference between what he called 'hot' media and 'cool' media, the former demanding much less from the viewer than the latter in terms of effort exerted in order to make meaning after. Although he also discussed comic books in his analysis of 'cool' media, television illustrated his points most clearly. For more see Marshall McLuhan, *Understanding Media: The Extensions of Man*. 1st ed. New York: McGraw-Hill, 1964, pp. 39–47.
2. Fiske argued that viewers of television held an active role in constructing meaning and pleasure; in other words, viewers worked with producers of television to make viewing a culturally significant practice. To read his description of this in full form, please see John Fiske, 'TV: Re-situating the Popular in the People', *Continuum: The Australian Journal of Media & Culture* 1:2 (1987), http://wwwmcc.murdoch.edu.au/ReadingRoom/1.2/Fiske.html.
3. Guy DeBord explains this all-encompassing characteristic of spectacle in the following way: 'The Spectacle is essentially tautological, for the simple reason that its means and its ends are identical. It is the sun that never sets on the empire of modern passivity. It covers the entire globe, basking in the perpetual warmth of its own glory.' Guy DeBord, *The Society of the Spectacle*, trans. Donald Nicholson-Smith. New York: Zone Books, 1995, p. 15.

Chapter 5

Stars, Mickey Mouse and the Ledge of Tomorrow

At the entrance of Disneyland there is a small plaque that reads 'Here you leave today and enter the world of yesterday, tomorrow, and fantasy'. Amazing really, that in these thirteen words we find the stuff of every child's dreams, of every adult's fantasy, of a country's sticky sweet mythology. Wrapped up in this sentence is a history of illusion, family vacations, honeymoons, crying children, 3 million hotdogs, ice-cream cones and many, many souvenirs bought and forgotten. To the postwar culture of the 1950s, this plaque works as a salve, a mending point articulated by a showman who had come to represent all that American joy could be. To a more cynical culture, these words are a sales pitch. A brand. A marketing tool for a company that brings in, according to several websites, over 56 billion dollars a year with its theme parks, movie theatres, hotels, restaurants, stuffed animal lines and DVD sales. But for us in the pessimistic mood, Walt Disney and his worlds will always be a source of tension. Because when we were younger, Disney World was our Mecca. We thought that entering that world kept us away from our own world. We watched Walt Disney on Sunday nights, hoping for a Donald Duck cartoon before the long movie that our parents seem to like more than us. The tension comes today, as we survey a world that needs much more than imagination. A world that needs to be released of its fantasy, of its showmanship.

After reading the words on the plaque at Disneyland's entrance a couple of times, it becomes evident that its sentiment completely annihilates the present. It shoves it off, places it in a container to be picked up as you leave the park, left to sit and stew in its own insistence on the immediacy of time and space. And in some ways, this is a fine action to take. We all need to leave ourselves and our worlds for while. We need to do this in order to understand the quality of our own experience – absence makes the heart, and the life, grow fonder. The problem occurs when this absence takes on a reality of its own, when being away becomes a state of being itself. Surely, departure of any kind, especially when it occurs on the plane of reality, has been a cultural yearning for almost any generation. For the 1950s it was leisure time, wrapped up in Coney Island and colour television. For the 1960s and 70s it was music, revolution and drugs. (And don't forget sex, yet that has its place for all generations and their hopes of escape.) In the 1980s it was money, in the 1990s it was flannel and the stock market, and today it is the air we breathe. All forms of escape, all forms of absence. Sometimes temporary, sometimes constant. This is what Elvis Presley sang for, what Allen Ginsberg howled about, what Kurt Cobain died for. Escape, and our desire for it.

It is this absence from reality, what Eco called 'hyperreality', that Walt Disney made corporate.[1] He industrialized the process of escapism. Look back at our lists of absences and notice that Disney was always there. And if he was always there to entertain, we might also ask what else he was doing? This is tricky, because when something is ever-present it is also invisible. Invisible yet there, subconscious, some philosophical system that hopes and prays to remain stealthily inconspicuous. So invisible that when it causes us to form understandings of gender, sexuality, race, wealth, class, violence, the different, the Other and all such things, we really don't see it at all. Snow White, Cinderella, Ariel, Pocahontas, all waiting to be rescued, but never rescuing themselves. The Wicked Witch, Medusa, Cruella Deville, all branding the bitch of sexuality. And the men, oh the wonderful men! Heroes, knights in shining armour, midgets, big-jawed jingoists. They were all well suited to destroy the different, the hunchback, the disabled. Such a wonderful cast of characters, casting our characters at the drop of a hat.

Stuart Hall would ask us to remember that Disney, in all its forms of production, operates as an encoding system – as an ideological Gatling gun, spewing bullets of vision and meaning for us to be penetrated by.[2] And while he would hope that we the viewer, the consumer, the digester would have enough cultural capital to oppose this system, we must admit that we are primarily dominated by this rodent-run hegemony. The warm glow of comfort that pours out of every Disney pore is not well suited for critical thinking, but for naps. Think about *Mary Poppins*. All is well, medicine is taken, penguins are danced with and then the film lullabies you to sleep with the dark, almost haunting scenes of the bag lady feeding the pigeons in the city square. It is this sadness, this melancholy, that drifts beneath the surface of all things Disney. And it has to be there in order for the ending to bring us back to the alternative reality and escape of splendour. It is certainly a formula that is not new for any Hollywood film, pop culture novel or music video. It's just that Disney has done it so well it appears seamless, which in the end makes that which we should be sceptical of that much more salient.

The year is 1989. Enter Britney Spears, eight years old at an audition for the new Mickey Mouse Club, a show at the centre of the newly formed Disney Channel. I like to imagine this first entry into the Disney world as an actual entrance into Disney World. A sort of common-day allegory in which the Princess pays for her entrance ticket with years of rehearsal time, practising at the evening church services, singing pop standards in the garage when the other kids were playing with the Slip 'n' Slide. Her ticket is punched by the mouse himself, smiling that fake smile from ear to ear. Her mother is there with her, holding her hand reminding her to keep smiling, keep it fresh. They walk up the steps of the Magic Kingdom, this icon of Disney reality, and young Britney is caught in a centrifuge of mixed realities. This is the kingdom, the one and only place that she will meet her maker. But just which maker she does not know yet – God or Walt. Thy kingdom come, thy will be done, on earth, in Orlando, Florida, as it is in heaven.

Actually, it would have been a sort of heaven for young Britney. A place where everything smells new, where memories are realities, where fantasy and fiction become truth. More importantly, this would be the place where she would finally find her purpose. This would be the place where all of her hard work would finally pay off, where she would be rewarded. And yet in 1989, the doors of heaven were not opened for her – she was not ready. Officials at Disney felt she was too young. Crushed by the news, young Britney turns around to retrace her moments-earlier triumphant ascension. Yet on her way out she and her mother are approached by a Disney executive not at the audition, let's call him Goofy. He wobbles over to the pair, giggles and drools, and suggests that she hook up with his New York agent friend, call him Donald, and start some professional training in performance. Without Goofy and Donald, no Britney Spears. Donald quacks his way through the New York celebrity system in order to find just the right place for young Britney to make her entry. And he finds help from another character, Ed McMahon.

The first episode of *Star Search* aired on 17 September 1983. On that show, a young Sharon Stone was competing in the model category. She would go on to show the world her crotch in the film *Basic Instinct*. Eight years later, a ten-year-old Britney Spears would perform on the show in the singing category. She would go on to show the world her crotch in the front seat of an SUV. Coincidence? Maybe.

In her performance of the song 'Love Can Build a Bridge', Britney actually sounds good, much better than most ten –year olds at least. She is wearing a tight black outfit with a huge white bow for shoulder pads, complemented by a white skirt. Her hair is curly, her make-up is awkward and her teeth poke out a bit. This performance would have been two years after her denial of entry into the Kingdom, and she had obviously done her work. If you watch the clip you might be surprised. I was for two reasons. First, there is much more soul in this little woman than there would ever be in the bigger woman that we have come to know as Britney Spears. At one point in the song, at the bridge, she growls into a note that honestly reminded me of a young Stevie Wonder. Certainly, the schmaltz factor is there. However, I still step back a bit and wonder about how this gospel note made it into her little vocal cords? The second thing to surprise me was the lack of sexuality in the performance. She is ten years old singing about lost love, but there is nothing sexual here. Margo Jefferson has written about how Michael Jackson, even in his younger years, exuded a sort of sexuality.[3] That is not present in Britney's performance on *Star Search*. Why am I surprised by this? Because in almost every other representation of Britney from that moment on there is always a whisper of sexuality.

Britney Spears loses on *Star Search* to a twelve year old named Marty Thomas. But did she really lose? Is there any sense of loss when you have made it onto a nationally televised program, even for five minutes? By this time Britney was starring in TV commercials, playing small roles in off-Broadway shows and singing on any county fair's stage that would take her. It's astonishing to think about what loss, real loss, meant to her in these younger years. Her train of fame was pushing forward so quickly that loss never really had a chance to sink its teeth into her. And maybe, just maybe, this was the problem. With mom pushing so hard to get Britney to the next level was there any time for her to actually sit and contemplate anything, let alone being a loser? Remember that Britney was anointed at a young age in her church, she was commissioned by God to be something special. This could not be taken away by Disney, Ed McMahon or anything.

And so, in 1992, when Britney re-auditioned for Disney's Mickey Mouse Club and got it, she was probably not surprised. Thrilled, certainly, but not surprised. Consider what Disney finally was offering her (or what they were not offering her). As a ten year old, Britney had tasted fame. She knew all of the backstage rituals, how to pose for the camera, how to speak in front of a microphone, how to use stage lights and sound systems, how to act during interviews, what clothes to wear, what clothes not to wear, how to intensify cuteness when it needed to be, how to act tough around other minor celebrities. Disney was not offering her any of this as new. In fact, her new job as a Mouseketeer actually only offered her consistency. Rather than travel from cultural stage to cultural stage, Britney was now able to secure her footing on a televised platform that would remain fixed. And remember that this show would not cater to the normal channel surfers of the early 1990s. Disney was cultivating a fixed audience, a collective of kids that would rearrange schedules, put off homework to watch their favourite show with their favourite kids being who they wanted to be. Disney had learned from MTV that children are the most lucrative market to tap into, due mainly to the fact that they are so devoted. Economically and socially devoted. Certainly, the Disney Channel had things to teach MTV as well; it just seems that when watching the new Mickey Mouse club there is a music video mentality that filled the space between the terrible skits acted by terrible actors.

This music video aesthetic is an odd thing to witness when it is removed from the MTV context. When watching MTV's video aesthetic, it makes sense to see people dancing around, lip-synching, rubbing against each other, pouting for the camera. It makes sense to see commercials as programming. But when we watch a video aesthetic on the Disney Channel the rules change a bit. The context of Disney adds the odd element of family values to an otherwise valueless text, the music video. But maybe considering them as valueless is not the right way to think about it. Instead, consider the Disney music video as a differently valued text. We may also be tempted to think about these Disney Channel videos in a manner that does not see them as primarily platforms of commerce. Again, we would be wrong in this assumption. The Disney Channel music video, like the MTV video, is indeed pitching something for a consumer. As I watch these episodes (painfully) it becomes glaringly clear that Britney Spears, Justin Timberlake, Christina Aguilera and the others who we don't know, are ambassadors of a certain type of experience. Pushing further, they are selling American youths the American youth experience – fun, puppy love, goofing around, white, middle class, free of real conflict, free of actual thought. These are the values of the Disney Channel, and these are the tools that young Britney was trained with.

But what is so wrong about a children's show pushing these sorts of values? Why is Disney at fault here? Or even Britney? Children's television should be about fun and American values, right? Certainly, on one level, nothing is wrong with this type of programming. It's silly, goodhearted and for some kids very entertaining. And children's television has always been part of the family structure. Bozo the clown made his way into my living room after a long day at school; Kukla, Fran and Ollie entertained my parents when they were children, and so on. Oscar the Grouch, Big Bird, Bert and Ernie, Speed Racer, Tom and Jerry, and the Flintstones have all had their place in our 'family structure'. They have been present and have not done that much harm.

But a discussion of Britney Spears and her relationship with the Disney folks isn't really about censorship, episodic criticism or whether or not children's television is worth it. That's another discussion. What matters is the way in which Britney was employed, for the first time, by an ideological system. Not only that, but by one which had by that time firmly grasped the imagination of an entire world. It is important for us to see this first process of use. Britney and the other Mouseketeers were asked to represent a certain type of childhood, one intermingled with cultural meaning and societal structures. When Britney sang for the Disney Channel, when she danced with her fellow child stars, when she made corny jokes about 'real life' matters, she was not actually Britney Spears. Instead, she was Disney Britney, a new sort of character that we might find stumbling through the hot August humidity in Disney World itself. She was, for the first time, an institutionalized structure. This was the beginning. The creation.

As a representation, Britney did very well. The programme itself did not, and was cancelled two years after she had been cast. But the work had been done. Britney the star had been created, pulled down from the cosmos of ordinariness and shot back up into a reality that would forever change her world. But do not forget that she was a representation, a facsimile of something grand, hip and fun. By this time, even at age ten or eleven, the real Britney had been tucked away. What we got was wrapped up in Disney wrapping paper. It would take her at least a couple more years to unwrap herself, or least another representation of herself, for some new consumption.

I have a good friend who grew up in Orlando. For his summer work in high school and college he worked at Disney World as a character actor, but not one in a suit. Instead, every day he got up and put a bandana on his head, an eye patch on his eye, and played a pirate for the Jungle Cruise. He never wanted to be in the suit, actually playing one of the famous characters for the kids. When I heard this I thought he was crazy. Why wouldn't you want to be the object, the spectacle of everybody's imagination and attention? He had a great answer. He told me that each character, like Mickey Mouse, was assigned a 'helper'. These helpers weren't really helpers at all, but bodyguards. It turns out that kids, mostly in their teen years, get a kick out of kicking the characters, trying to get them to come out of character. The goal is getting Mickey or Goofy to cuss them out in front of all the adoring fans.

Disney was the first to put Britney in the suit. It would take us a couple more years to start kicking. And when we did, we kicked her off the ledge of tomorrow, and she fell straight into us.

Notes

1. Umberto Eco, *Travels in Hyperreality*. Orlando: Harcourt Brace & Company, 1986, pp. 5–6.
2. Stuart Hall identifies a complex system by which to understand the way meaning is made through media. He explains that mediated messages are 'encoded' by producers of, say, films. It is our job (most times unconsciously so) to 'decode' those messages based on social, cultural and political factors. For a complete explanation of this process see Stuart Hall, 'Encoding/Decoding'. In Paul Marris and Sue Thornham, *Media Studies: A Reader*. 2nd ed. New York: New York University Press, 2000, pp. 51–61.
3. Margot Jefferson, *On Michael Jackson*. New York: Vintage Books, 2007, pp. 67–69.

Part II

Consumption

Chapter 6

The Universal Woman, Saint or Whore?

> *The characteristics of the Eternal Woman are opposed to those of a developing, authentic* person, *who will be unique, self-critical, self-creating, active and searching.*
>
> Mary Daly[1]

In January of 1999, producer Max Martin released the record '... Baby One More Time' on Jive Records. Singing on the record, of course, was Britney Jean Spears, the once Mouseketeer, once *Star Search* star, once little girl from The South. This album would be the start of something big for Britney, the platform on which her career would stand, the beginning of a global phenomenon that would, in time, call to question issues of sexuality, appropriateness, fan culture, women's rights, pornographic photographs, regional heritage, capitalism and consumption itself. But this CD would also be the end of things: privacy, the potential of innocence, middle-class living, personally censored sexuality, ownership of gender, ownership of anything, really – all lost upon the release of this monstrosity of a CD.

The CD itself really wasn't the start. It was the music video for the title track that got the ball rolling. This is the video everyone from MTV jockeys to Diane Sawyer was talking about. The infamous Catholic school girl vignette that initiated Britney's enormous step away from what she once was toward the thing she would become. Like most videos from the late 90s, there isn't much of a story here. The narrative of the video hangs on a thin tale in which young Britney laments the loss of a boyfriend, pictured as a hunky basketball player, whom she lost because she wasn't paying attention. She is pictured in the video as a forbidden fruit, a sixteen-year-old vamp that certainly would hold the attention of any young suitor.

But video narrative wasn't ever going to be the focus for Britney Spears products. In fact, storyline was only there as another vehicle to show off a body, a sexuality, a persona. And so the true value of the first video seems to be its introduction of Britney the new body, the new attitude. And the camera goes a long way towards making this introduction.

Follow the first frames of the video – the camera dollies through the legs and ankles of bored girls and boys waiting patiently for the final class bell to ring. The camera doesn't stop until he gets to the most shapely legs in the class (it's a gendered camera, don't fool yourself). He stops and glances up the legs to find a skirt that barely covers the girl underneath it. He pauses, allowing a good look. Perhaps the most important millisecond of Britney's career, or at least the most titillating up to that moment. Remember, this girl had never been shown this way, had never invited this sort of glance or vantage point. Hungry for more, the camera flips to the desktop where it finds young Britney, chewing gum through very pouty, red lips. She twiddles a pencil, her hair perfect. She is the schoolgirl, yet not at all like any of the schoolgirls at home watching the video after school. In fact, there is such a divide between Britney and her viewer that the latter's attention confuses me even now.

While she was a Mouseketeer, Britney might have appeared to be just like Jenny, Emily, Katie or any of her fans. Indeed, that was probably her appeal to the folks running the Disney Channel. Here was an American girl – blonde hair, blue eyes, middle-class smile – it was all there. So when girls watched Britney on TV they could easily project themselves into the scenarios. They were on television – well, kind of. At least it could have been them, could have become them. In this way, our three girls were choosing their star rather than Disney making the selection for them. They were empowered, as much as they could be at that age, to anoint their queen. Britney was a success story scraped out of the experiences they were having. She was the chosen one, chosen by them for them. They were part of the creation process.

But their connection to their creation was altered with the video for this first single. The marionette strings were untangled from their sticky fingers and given to the power players of Jive Records. Sure, the context was still there, but everything else was different. Katie could project herself into the Catholic school when Britney chewed her gum, but really the connection ended there. The legs, hair, perfect make-up, clothing and dance moves all worked as an odd barrier between her and her queen. The video is an invitation that quickly turns into a refusal, a denial, a conclusion. It shouldn't come as a surprise to understand that all music videos in one way or another work as a sort of refusal. They are fantastic invitations but in the end always a reminder of reality – ours not theirs. Michael Jackson videos were always like this – I could buy the zippered, fake red leather jacket at Kmart, I could learn the lyrics, I could gel my hair, I could even buy the sequinned glove, but in the end, I could never fully transport myself to the world of the video. I could not dance with those people, I could never get the moves just right and I could never be in the 'danger zone' of the fake streets. And this was the case for Jenny, Emily and Katie when they watched Britney's first video. They could only get so far, and then came the scenes of the dancing stomach.

Britney's stomach nestled between the plaid, Catholic skirt and the white, tied-up oxford shirt seemed to be the target for people worried about this video and folks who loved the video alike. For the worriers, the stomach was just too much – too much skin, too much body, too close to the private myths of sexuality. No girl of this age should show that kind of stomach to anyone, even their family. For the new fans, the stomach was everything. Trained by years of sexual advertisements, these eyes knew well the stomach that was given to them. But actually, the enduring quality of Britney's tummy for these folks was that it wasn't actually given, but dangled in front of them; it was almost offered, almost presented, forbidden yet on display. When any youthful female body is sexualized in front of a camera you will find this twofold reaction. On one hand you find the protectors, those who would offer a cover-up to young girls who find their bodies on display. On the other hand you find the cover-up artists, arguing that she, the naked woman (not girl) made the choice to be on display, to be out there in the open for all to see. We can now call this the Madonna syndrome.

Roughly fifteen years before Britney dances in her Catholic skirt, a young woman from Detroit began blazing a trail for young female musicians and artists. Britney would kiss this woman on stage several years later, a kiss that I often thought of as a thank-you kiss – a sort of wet endorsement. The rhetoric swarming around Madonna at the time of her anointing is quite similar to that which we find working itself around Britney in 1999, and almost identical to contemporary discussions about Lady GaGa. Scholarship and criticism about Madonna deals with the same debate: is she being exploited or is she exploiting herself?[2] At the final count, those who empowered her as someone who exploited herself for money and power have won the battle. Madonna knows exactly what she's doing, still to this day. And she has done it well. So the Madonna syndrome opens the door to the argument that Britney, even in this first video, knew exactly what she was doing. She was in charge, she was the one inviting the camera up her skirt. Certainly, for anyone making money on Britney, this line of argument is very attractive. But it is also delusional. It is a marketing explanation rather than a cultural or personal one. It is an argument that you can make about a woman in her 30s. It is not, however, an argument that we could make about Britney in 1999. Nor can we make it today. Self-exploitation requires self-knowledge. The village spectacle must never know that she is a spectacle, or else the game is up.

The last two and a half minutes of the video are rather stock. In other words, they are less interesting in terms of understanding the true meaning or value of the text itself. This final part of the video shows our queen dancing, singing to the camera, fondling a basketball. It is the first minute and a half that really holds the pendulum power, the swing that would change the manner in which America would consume the body of Britney. And to me, it is the Catholic skirt, the Catholic outfits, the Catholic context that deserves attention. It is here where we might become aware of the presence of another madonna, The Madonna, the mother of Jesus Christ. This Madonna operates as the universal woman or, according to feminist theologian Mary Daly, at least half of the universal woman available to Christian women. The other half of the universal woman is Eve, the Apple biter, or conversely Mary Magdalene, the prostitute who followed Jesus. The universal woman is therefore a dichotomy – one part St Mary the other part Evil Eve, one part virgin the other part whore.[3] And so, within the context of Catholic theology, Daly points out that women were urged to pick St Mary as their ideologue, as their one image. Having children, being a portal for birthing more Catholics, was the primary use of women. This was the identity to yearn for, to pray for. Mary Magdalene, and all the things wrapped up within this half of the sacred woman, was the part of the universal woman that you prayed not to become; pray against sexuality, immorality, potential. Don't get caught with your skirt around your ankles but instead get caught in the kitchen.

These sorts of spiritual identities are embedded in the Britney Spears video introduction. The video for '… Baby One More Time' unwittingly plays with the presentation of a universal woman. And I do think that by this time we need to call her a woman. It is too difficult not to do so. Because the sexuality that swims through this text, if actually applied to a girl like your little sister or daughter or niece, would haunt you. What the video does is actually ask an important question regarding the universal woman: will Britney be saint or whore? What do we want her to be? What do we want her to become?

Note that this is exactly the question that her producers want us to ask. In other words, this is the tension always brought out by sexuality, youth and their fusion inside popular culture. As female stars got younger and younger, it was this tension upon which they tiptoed into success. Remember Debbie Gibson and Tiffany? They sang about love, the puppy sort. They sang about broken hearts, about first kisses, about being alone for the first time with a boy. Lyrics are quite different by the time Britney emerges. But what is also different is that Debbie Gibson and Tiffany were not as young as Britney. They were not offered as children; they were young adults, fully clothed. This didn't stop viewers from having crushes on them. But it may have stopped the severity of those crushes, the intensity of the pleasures offered by their bodies. Britney was a new phenomenon, a new type of child offering. And, more to the point, a new sort of product. One that was cultivated from a young age, harvested from new soil, picked a little too early. And herein lies the tension, the two-sided dichotomy of the universal woman. This 'too young' side of Britney is the St Mary, the innocent, the perfect. The mature side, the ripe side, is the damsel, the sexual side of female identity, the one that is dangerous. And when these two sides work together they can make some serious cash. Because, of course, this is what producers were planning on. They want us to feel something. For young girls and young boys, excitement is enough. But for adults, they need feelings that are more complex. They need us as well as the kids to feel something. And if that something is doubt, guilt, confusion or tension, then they have us.

The tension of the universal woman is really a tension steeped in questions which are never asked. In what ways do we see the universal woman – how is she represented to us? What is the value of a female life? Where does the woman begin to find herself, her identity? Who is in control of the universal woman – God? Man? Certainly not women, right? Can the universal woman be changed, altered, reformed?

If Britney Spears is the universal woman, all of these questions must be asked for her, about her.

These are the questions that we need to begin asking if we are to understand this first video from Britney. These are the questions that the producers don't want us to ask, again not wanting us to think but only to feel. And in some ways, they've put their money in the right place. We won't ask these questions. Why would we? For example, none of us would think to wonder about why Britney Spears, this Southern Baptist Christian, would make her music video debut in a stereotypically Catholic outfit. Certainly, Southern Baptist religion falls under the holy Catholic church in some way or another, but not in the American imagination. Catholics are one type of faith folks, Baptists are another. And yet here is Britney essentially posing as both. On the American screens of popular culture, Catholicism represents a certain, recognizable type of American religion. But when Britney is shown as a Catholic schoolgirl there is a multilayered fulfilment, one that goes beyond national identity. On one level, being a Catholic schoolgirl, in a Catholic schoolgirl outfit, fulfills a fantasy that has been around for a long time: Catholic equals good, schoolgirl equals innocent; Catholic schoolgirl equals the perfect ironic and paradoxical impression of sexuality just waiting to happen. On another level, Britney in a Catholic schoolgirl outfit marks her not only as a sexual body but also a classed body. In the outfit, Britney is drenched with middle-class experience, with private education, with proper life. And yet, the tension is still there. For what better place is there for a sexual escapade then middle America?

So ask some of the questions that the universal woman brings out in a discussion of Britney Spears. What is the value of Britney? How does the video answer such a question? The value of a woman in the context of this music video is caught somewhere between being sexual and being romantic, being a tart and being a lonely girlfriend, being a person and being a body. In the first minute and a half Britney is sex dancing in a school hallway. Later in the video she is a cute girl, playing with friends, doing cartwheels in the parking lot of some urbanized space, singing in a 1950s convertible. But all of these 'classical' images are drawn from the pen of the preceding images. The final answer to what kind of woman Britney is becomes much more convoluted than you would imagine. The value of Britney is thus a multiple value. In short, she is an open text, a canvas on which we and the producers can do our work. As such, the created value of Britney is not innate. Like the beginnings of any star's identity, Britney's is a patchwork quilt that, while including some of her own work, is mostly filled and stuffed with the work of others. The value is communal, but in the worst sense of the word.

Another question: where does Britney become aware of her own identity? Painted as the universal woman, a female has little opportunity for awareness of any kind let alone that of the self. Perhaps more fairly, a theology of universalism does offer a sort of identification but, as we have pointed out, a very limited one. You may be one of two things: a mother of no one, stained with sexual sin; or, you may be the mother of one, the victor of history. Which one is Britney? More importantly, what role does she have in choosing? Present only as the subject of the pop culture industry, this first video operates on the level of metaphor – as a product of the Kingdom of Pop, Britney is a ward of the state, a pawn for the majesty. Consequently, she has no role in deciding what her identity will be. She just is. And while I think we can argue about whether or not this changes as she gets older, for now we must remain alongside the performer in the video. This is our subject, she is our subject. She is our object, to put it more correctly. And as an object she has very little to say about who she actually is, about what her identity will be seen as, and about what she wants to be by herself. The truth is she will never be, after this video, by herself. Her constant companions, the camera, the fan, the overbearing mother, the money, the contracts, the interviewer, the journalists, the make-up artists, the athletic trainer, the dietitian, will always be there. A sort of awkward and ironic isolation which is never isolating yet always marginalizing.

In other words, the question about who is in control of this universal woman requires many answers. The inch of hope and optimism that we might have about Britney Spears will urge us to say that she plays a small part in the control. Yet honesty nudges us towards other sorts of answers. We are in control, the producers (who are mostly men), are in control, and God, well, he seems to be a little bit absent here. It is this last answer that gets most complicated when we think about theology and Britney. The God that Britney believes in, that her family believes in, steps into life through the Holy Spirit. In other words, he is actively involved with his creation, inspiring their very existence. The God of Catholicism, or to be more precise Roman Catholicism, is not as actively involved with his people. He is present, yet mediated for by priests, saints and architecture. This difference with Southern Baptist belief is quite illuminating as we follow our inspection of the universal woman. As a Catholic girl, one interpretation might be that Britney is not immediately owned or manufactured by the laws of God, but by the laws of God's people. A sort of middle ground before purgatory is where we find Britney dancing in the hallways of the Catholic high school. As a Baptist, there is no video. As a Baptist, perhaps there isn't even a career. But posing as a good Catholic schoolgirl, hovering over the imagination of a culture predetermined to understand her as a symbol of good or evil, Britney is right where she needed to be.

And this is where she would stay as a consumable product for a good while. Any alterations, reformations or changes to this universal woman would have to come much later in her life. And even then, the ownership of such reformation must still be questioned. Keep an eye out for the role God plays here. Like many celebrities who have fallen out of grace, Britney will be grabbing at grace like straws in an afternoon contest between siblings who don't want to clean up after the dog in the backyard. Short straw picks up. Long straw gets to go free.

Notes

1. Mary Daly, *The Church and the Second Sex.* New York: Harper & Row, 1968, pp. 106–107.
2. Some of the early, and unfortunately best scholarship on Madonna is out of print. However, the following sources point to some stellar interpretation of her work and its political and aesthetic consequences: Santiago Fouz-Hernáandez and Freya Jarman-Ivens, eds, *Madonna's Drowned Worlds: New Approaches to Her Cultural Transformations.* Burlington: Ashgate Publishing Company, 2004; Georges-Claude Guilbert, *Madonna as Postmodern Myth: How One Star of Self-Construction Rewrites Sex, Gender, Hollywood and the American Dream.* Jefferson: McFarland & Company, 2002; Karlene Faith, *Madonna: Bawdy and Soul.* Toronto: University of Toronto Press, 1997.
3. The work of Mary Daly has profound importance on the creation of a liberatory theology for women in the Catholic church. Inspired by the work of Simone de Beauvoir, Daly was one of the first women to challenge what she saw as a 'symbolic theology', one in which women were translated from real human beings into symbolic images of inspiration (i.e. St Mary, mother of God) or scorn (i.e. prostitute, Mary Magdalene) (Daly 1968, pp. 114–115).

Chapter 7

A New Currency

Between 1999 and 2008 Britney Spears made a lot of money. Miriam Datskovsky, an economics reporter for Portfolio.com, estimates that 'the Britney Spears economy', which would include monies made through magazine sales, perfume sales, record sales, public appearances, advertising deals, etc. has an annual value of $120 million. Since her debut in 1999, she has sold 83 million records, bringing in roughly $400 million for Jive Records. Her tour profits, which include tickets and merchandise, have made roughly $150 million (Britney's promotion company makes over $500,000 for each night she performs). The most astonishing figure in Datskovsky's report is that Britney's management gets paid between $250,000 and $400,000 for Britney to show up at a party or an event. In the end, according to court documents, Britney herself brings in approximately $737, 000 a month, which averages out to about $9 million a year. Her net worth is roughly $125 million.

I will limit myself to only a couple of comments from the many that could be made about these dollar amounts. First, that Britney makes this much money is as striking as the fact that she *only* makes this much money. For most of us $125 million is a whole lot of dough. On the other hand, for what she has given us, this seems like chump change. Second, the amount of money made by Britney for other people seems to intensify the idea of her as a person being used. Let's not be ignorant – all celebrities are used by corporations and associations. Why expect anything different in the experiences of Britney? Indeed, this is the formula of the American economic system, and has been for decades. But it's more than just making money. Britney's being used in so many ways beyond this project of raising capital makes the process even more significant. Lastly, money can become as imperative as we want it to be in our understanding of how Britney operates as a cultural product. On one hand, we can fairly say that money is something that all celebrities swim in without noticing its presence on their skin. In other words, Britney's money has nothing to do with her exile. On the other hand, we might begin to question whether or not the presence of capital alters this young woman's desires, hopes, inner struggles, ambitions and purpose.

While difficult to do, we must be able to stand back and look at the issue of currency itself if we are to understand the way money makes its way into the story. And when currency enters any conversation, it complicates, rewrites and obliterates, because it is not simply compensation for work. Rather, it is a multi-headed beast that drools and spits in many forms. Currency operates on the levels of economy, culture, personal worth and self-understanding. Currency is the self, but particularly in the way that George Herbert Mead discussed the self.[1] He understood the self as a by-product of a manipulative act, as the stuff of human consciousness, action and attention. In other words, the self for Mead is much more than just the inner workings of the brain. Instead it is an amalgam of a collective. It is a combination of inner values brought on by the interaction of the self and society. It is in this way that the self is currency. The self is the earnings of living among others. A new sort of currency emerges here, one that illuminates the inner workings of a life spent in public.

The currency of Britney Spears certainly involves capital, but not simply the green kind. It involves sexual capital, social capital, cultural capital, star capital and so on. The psychological and emotional weight of these multiplicities of capital allow a more nuanced understanding of how the idea of 'worth' itself gets unpacked in the archaeological work of digging up the Britney story. It changes the way we define the Britney economy. And the digging changes everything – money is no longer the only source of value here. Money becomes a part of the complicated puzzle of the value of a woman captured in the constellations of the American star system.

But, in order to please the economic pragmatists in the audience, we can start by looking at money, the first piece, a corner piece. Cash changes everything – look at the faces of those lucky bastards who win state lotteries. They remind me of silly putty gone warm, when the expressions and contours of the clay become unrecognizable even to those who own it. The cheeks, chubby and red from smiling a new way, are transformed globular flesh. They are newly formed, newly shaped by money. And the eyes are also telling. Look at the unexpected joy, the hidden greed of being able to buy anything you want, the freedom from work that the eyes hold in the gaze of glee. I think I see some of this in the Mouseketeer Britney. At that time, though not making much money compared to what she would, young Britney was no doubt feeling some splendour from the spending cash offered by the mouse. And yet, because her parents were involved so closely with her career at this stage, there would have been some class-centered rhetoric anchoring the whole situation, a sort of 'don't forget where you come from' mantra. Proof of this is in the accent that we still hear when Britney is on camera for the Disney Channel. The southern accent was a selling point certainly, but also a way for Britney and her family to remain real, connected, trapped by their regional, lower-middle-class stamp. Be the heroes of your town, be the example for others to strive for, be what they will never be. While they are stuck in the dust of a town, you are jumping from the stars of the city. But you're still them in the end. Never lose that.

When was it finally lost? When was this connection, this anchoring, stripped off for something much newer and more fragrant? For post-Disney Britney the money must have been so much more exciting, so much heavier. It operated as a departure ticket, as a first-class ticket out of second class, the middle class of America. And with this sort of upgrade comes a shift of sensibilities, a shift of self-understanding that certainly all celebrities must bear. The money holds one hand while the other hand waves goodbye to macaroni and cheese, to picnics at the park, to Sunday barbecues, to sleepovers with ratty old sleeping bags, to sweat pants. All of these things would make it back into Britney's story yet in a different, manipulative way. By the time they make it back into her life, these things are desperate calls for normalcy. They are spectacles of memories. But in 1999 and 2000, they were things she used to do, used to eat, used to be.

But it would be a mistake to say that Britney and her money simply ushered her into the upper class. Instead her buckets of cash made her classless. A sort of transcendental state of income had replaced what was once a budgeted class. There are no piggy banks in the classless heaven, no money management, no coupons. In fact, in a sort of paradoxical way there is no money at all. Britney's fingers never touched a bill, never felt the surface of a coin dropped into a machine for a soda, the smooth folds of a five dollar bill spent on a pair of socks. She never wrote a check, never slid a credit card through machine, never snapped closed a billfold again. Those tactile pleasures of money are removed in the classless existence. They are either felt by fingers who work for her or completely digitized by the ever-growing organization, the Britney Corporation. What sort of reality is that? What does it feel like to have money become the air you breathe, the sweat you exude, the stuff of your space? We can imagine exhilaration, a feeling of immortality, of freedom. But we can also imagine a world of anxiety, of being out of control. The classless heaven is a lonely place filled with only others who are classless. In addition, being classless means that you are also diminished in other ways. It means saying goodbye to other friends who still need to save money to buy cars. It means pitching off a sense of fulfillment that comes from living well, within your means. Means are gone, out of your knowledge system. When you are classless you live by a different standard, one that segregates as much as it compensates. You are in the front of the bus, you are in the swanky culture clubs, you are invited to the party. But only you.

So much for the cash side of currency. The new currency that Britney Spears found herself in is also filled by the glances of society, the interaction outlined by Mead. Put devastatingly plainly, money was only one way in which Britney was reinventing herself. Her self was being reconstructed by the mere fact that she was noticeable. She was someone that people recognized as being wonderful, different, Other. I was at a conference once in Philadelphia, giving a paper on the films of Tod Browning. After my lecture, I was talking to a member of the audience who had a couple questions for me. After about five minutes, he looked down at my name tag and made the connection to my first book, an edited collection about cinematic representations of people with disabilities. He said that he had read the book and that it had changed his scholarly outlook on issues of minorities in the media. Maybe you have had one of these experiences yourself. When somebody recognizes you for the work you have done it feels good. You feel like you are walking out onto the stage into the bright spotlight of recognition. There is a warm feeling in your self-understanding that is intensified when these wonderful situations happen. For me, I was giddy. It made me feel good about me. When the world outside of me stops, opens the window, and yells 'hey, aren't you that guy?'

In 2000 Britney must've had at least 200 of these experiences each day. At a shopping mall, now the expensive one, being seen buying the things that only rich people can. In your car, always in your fancy car waving to the wavers on the sidewalk. At the hair salon. At the great smelling restaurants, in the hottest clubs, in your bathing suit. To be recognized is to be worked on by culture, by society. But in such a good way. To be noticed is to be dying to your older self and resurrected as something new. Canadian Philosopher Charles Taylor talks about the violent act of misrecognition placed upon minority cultures as being a social force equalled only by annihilation and extermination.[2] He is not actually talking about being recognized or not. He is talking about being recognized incorrectly as something much more abusive. To be painted incorrectly by the society of your self shatters the core of identity. When you are misrecognized you are caught under the thumb of the powerful, stuck within a context of complacency and barred from self-actualization's victory tune. So at the very moment that Britney begins to be noticed, recognized, she also finds herself chained to the whims of misrecognition.

But how do we come to gauge whether or not recognition, misrecognition or some combination of both was actually understood by her? At some primary level we might even question if celebrity is a sort of glamorized misrecognition. When people recognized Britney in 2000, who were they actually spotting? Put more accurately, what were they spotting? At the level of pure biological essentialism, they were noticing and recognizing the conglomeration of cells, skin, muscle and bone that reflected the symbol of Britney Spears. She was a person to be known. Of course, on a level of celebrity and cultural representation they were recognizing the star Britney Spears, the girl from the video, the girl with the voice and the hair and the boobs. Photographers from magazines and newspapers hunted for this entity. And when they found her and made their image we slurped up the acetate. Their recognition became our recognition which would in turn inspire us to recognize even more the beautiful, created currency of Britney Spears.

The recognition of Star Britney is not exactly the misrecognition that Taylor outlines in his politics of misrecognition. Or is it? This star recognition, this star currency, certainly brings joy, prestige and glamour to the young girl's life. In this sense it is positive, even desired. But by who? We've said before that fame certainly took hold of Britney at a very young age, to the point that she no doubt hungered it in all its forms – the stage, the television camera, the photo shoots, the magazine layouts, the recording studio. Note now that these are forms of recognition, avenues toward cultural currency. And so while she certainly desired this star recognition, alongside her, sharing in the joy and desire, was the machine of the Britney Corporation. All the many parts of her star-making machine had invested a lot of capital to gain cultural and social power in the name of Britney Spears. In reverse, looking away from the machine, how does young Britney look to them? This is where things get clarified, for it is from this vantage point that we begin to see misrecognition happening all over again to Britney Spears. Certainly in the front offices, in the coffee meetings, in the 'family time' of company parties, Britney was their daughter. They loved her, cared for her. But more than a daughter, she was their ticket to the big revenue.

And so while *celebrity* misrecognition, that form of noticing that we all participate in, operates in a very different cultural arena than Taylor originally mapped out, it is within what we might call *corporate* misrecognition that we find the bearer being oppressed. Operating as the Other in this context, Britney herself gets tagged with the label of currency – she is capital. And along with this new label, this new burden of misrecognition, comes two yokes that no young person's neck should ever have to carry: yokes of adult accountability and responsibility. In 2000, Britney Spears was eighteen years old. Remind yourself where you were when you were eighteen. Some of you may have been going to college for your freshman year, some working a full-time job and some of you may have been helping to raise a family. None of you were putting food on the table for more than 1,000 people with money you made while touring the globe. None of you were asked personal questions in front of millions about sexuality, chastity or plastic surgery. None of you were dressed by others who did not trust you to handle the expensive garments bought for you. None of you spent your free time in front of cameras, posing for yet another misrecognition moment. None of you were a corporation. None of you smelled like Britney Spears, worked like Britney Spears, did anything like Britney Spears.

These sorts of responsibilities, these manners of being held accountable, they are the oppressive devices of corporate misrecognition. Yet they are also a major source of currency for all celebrities. Britney had to juggle the responsibilities of an adult in order to secure a currency of an adult, albeit one wrapped in a childlike package. All celebrities, young or old, have to do this. Or at least that is what we have made them believe. The American culture system works under the assumption that while celebrities embody all of our dreams, they must suffer through all of our nightmares in order to get to that position. Britney teaches us this with clarity. Her celebrity is crafted into currency by other people, other than herself that is. Certainly she is the trigger, smooth and curved, ready for action. However it is the upstairs folks that oil the gun that they have forged from steel, fire and publicity.

Britney's new currency, new from the Mouseketeer age, new from *Star Search* days, new from her southern neighbourhoods, new from her old self, is a currency of cash, recognition, misrecognition and many, many more things:

The currency of evangelical Christianity
The currency of Republican politics
The currency of America itself

The currency of being a blonde, which connected her to Madonna, Marilyn Monroe, and others
The currency of The South
The currency of created innocence
The currency of Disney
The currency of the body, a perfect body
The currency of being young, alive and energetic
The currency of tight clothing
The currency of choreography
The currency of clean, straight teeth
The currency, eventually, of currency itself

I'm sure you will agree that while the contents of this list teach us a good deal, it is what's not on the list that really pulls eyelids apart:

The currency of self
The currency of authenticity
The currency of normalcy (define this as you wish)
The currency of being. Just being

Admittedly, the reason these four things are not on the list is that they are not, properly speaking, currency at all. Instead, they are essential bits of us that cannot be reformulated, packaged, sold and resold for the right price. They cannot wander off in hopes of finding something better. They are anchored to us by skin and bone. These are the things that are left out of the new currency of celebrity life, of American popular culture, of you and me. These are not merely images dancing on the cave wall for Plato and his prisoners.[3] These are things that we actually digest and keep.

Notes

1. George Herbert Mead, *Selected Writings*, Andrew J. Reck, ed. Chicago: University of Chicago Press, 1964, pp. 142–149.
2. Taylor describes the creation of identity as being anchored to the other, a sort of conversation between our inner thoughts and our impressions of, and interactions with, people around us: 'Thus my discovering my own identity doesn't mean that I work it out in isolation, but that I negotiate it through dialogue, partly overt, partly internal, with others. That is why the development of an ideal of inwardly generated identity gives a new importance to recognition. My own identity crucially depends on my dialogical relations with others.' As such, being 'misrecognized' has deep philosophical and political relationship with our connection to humanity itself. Charles Taylor et al., *Multiculturalism: Examining the Politics of Recognition*. Princeton: Princeton University Press, 1994, p. 34.
3. My understanding of this parable by Plato is greatly inspired by the late Susan Sontag. For her analysis please see Susan Sontag, *On Photography*. New York: Picador, 1973, pp. 3–26.

Chapter 8

Stuff

Kids these days don't play with dolls enough. Or action figures. It's all big stuff now, things with batteries, power cords, stuff that lights up. I don't think my son has a toy that doesn't make some sort of sound – most make me hum the tune of 'Old McDonald had a Farm' in inappropriate places. These toys spew out a different sort of sound than the toys I had when I was their age. To make my Bozo the Clown doll say something goofy, I simply pulled a string. No whistles, no bangs, no frills, just a funny voice that always made me laugh. Everything was simpler. I used to look through the plastic eyeball of my million-dollar man, Lee Majors. All of it was tactile, non-digital, so boring compared to the toys today, where the eyeball offers the three year old night vision. Preparing to be little soldiers. Today's toys, the digital ones, are actually making kids smarter. Or at least that is what media critic Steven Johnson argues.[1] He makes the point, somewhat convincingly, that gaming systems like the Wii or Sony PlayStation help children learn crucial mapping skills, resolution tactics and so forth. In other words, the lives they live in their digital hemisphere apparently prepare them for their corporeal one. My toys prepared me for nothing.

In the early 1980s, my favourite toy was a Paul Stanley doll from the Kiss action figure collection. I inherited it from my brothers who moved on from dolls to LP records and eight tracks when they became teenagers. The doll was about fifteen inches tall, dressed in spandex, donned in make-up and curly black hair. I would put on the *Kiss Alive!* album in my bedroom and make Paul dance to my favourite songs, 'Black Diamond' and 'Cold Gin'. I'd also gotten the record from my brothers. I always imagined that they would approve of this activity, but not the other stuff that Paul and I did. For example, Paul and I went to school together, talked during spelling lessons. We did recess together, lunchtime, bathroom time. He went with me to church, perhaps begrudgingly, but was always there singing the hymns with his pouty red lips. Paul went on vacation with me, went to friend's houses with me, walked around the neighbourhood with me. One memorable time he held a firecracker on a July evening. That was the end of our relationship and his torso.

Kiss were of course pioneers when it came to marketing products to children while at the same time singing songs about sex to adolescents.[2] And while most of the music was terrible people loved this group. And I think they loved them because they were portable, accessible and a little bit freaky. The Paul Stanley doll filled all of these criteria – it was miniature, easy to take around and always fuelled playtime with my friends. He became a sort of emblem for me, a way to show that I was into stuff older kids were into while at the same time meeting my desire to have a doll with me at all times. A rock 'n' roll security blanket.

Merchandising and rock 'n' roll music, or any popular music form, seems quite natural today. It started with Elvis – my aunt still has a 1958 calendar with his face on every month. And there were stickers, T-shirts, transistor radios, posters, all of which made the king of rock 'n' roll pliable. To be an Elvis fan was only partially about music, only somewhat about the sounds being made in Sun Studios in Memphis. The other parts, as we know, were physical (his body, its movement), commercial and communal. To love Elvis was to own Elvis. Thus is the lesson of merchandise, learned well by the proprietors of pop – give the kids a star in all its forms. Let them take him or her home in multiple packages. The people behind Michael Jackson, Madonna, New Kids on the Block, Menundo, Tiffany, Prince (the list goes on for a while), all understood that to make money in music meant to make money in plastic, fabric and buttons.

The manufacturing and merchandising of Britney Spears does not leave space for disappointment. By the middle of the 1990s, fans of Britney Spears had become collectors of Britney Spears. And all of their treasures are now available on eBay. Take a minute and enter Britney Spears in the search window of your eBay account. There are roughly two dozen categories of items that you can choose from in order to make your searches more precise – antiques, industrial products, music, memorabilia, etc. Of these categories, approximately five do *not* have Britney Spears products available. This is quite shocking if you consider that you can find Britney Spears industrial products like a mouse pad for your computer. There is Britney fine art, Britney clothing, Britney electronics, Britney soap, Britney perfume, Britney underwear, Britney posters, Britney autographs, Britney CDs, Britney rarities, and my favourite, Britney food.

Beyond the safe marketplace of eBay, there are of course other products, movies and images of Britney available. A sort of black market of pornography and sexual pleasure exists. This is the darker side of merchandising, that which moves beyond the hands of the pop proprietor. But we need to see this as commercial appropriation just the same, for it is a source of capitalism that the Internet has allowed since its inception.

These markets of Britney Spears merchandise tend to blend at the edges, creating a sort of fabric for sale. Money buys anything, but it also creates a space for anything. Products and services of all kind flood the space of a market, not only because people are trying to make money but also because people are willing to pay for just about anything. Certainly, the fabric of the marketplace thrives on the work of producers and buyers both. Yet it is important to note, as Max Weber did in 1904, that this fabric is not the work of one individual, or group of individuals. Rather the fabric of the Britney Spears marketplace is the outcome of an entire spirit of capitalism. Weber explains that while the genesis of capitalism can be found in the minds and pockets of who he called the 'heroic entrepreneurs', its lifeblood actually comes from a spirit or zeitgeist which has been agreed upon by a society.[3] Thus capitalism and its support of the Britney market cannot solely be placed in the hands of her producers or her consumers, or even her. Rather, the transfer of Britney Spears to merchandise is a philosophical, political and economic imagination event.

We might liken this imagination of capitalism to any other communal permission project. For example, why do we believe that every child deserves educational opportunities? Why do we think these opportunities come in eight-hour slices of our weekly lives? Why did we choose to teach our children one version of history (of winners) versus another (of losers)? Why is formalized education compulsory? Many of us could not answer these questions, yet our actions and money are wrapped up in our underlying beliefs about the issues surrounding public education. We might say that compulsory education is simply a moral good, a way to support and sustain our society. But even this is not a justified answer, a blanket statement that all could define together in the same way. Thus, instead of some signed-on-the-dotted-line cultural contract regarding education we have instead a shared imagination about why it is important and who deserves it. This imagination is binding in that it guides our social action, but it is imaginary just the same. Such is the case with our imagination about capitalism.

But how does this imagination come to justify the merchandising of an individual? To answer this perhaps we first need to identify what happens when a person, a real-life, breathing body, becomes a product for sale. It's cute, on the surface, that there are Britney Spears key chains, Britney clothing, Britney perfume, Britney dolls. But enough of cuteness for the time being – take a deeper breath of this capital air.

A first step is to grapple with the idea of likenesses and reproductions. We all have been likened, but we usually call it impression. When someone takes your photograph they are taking your likeness and impressing it upon film, digital mapping or otherwise. Thus our impressions or our likenesses clutter our homes, Facebook pages, cell phones and hard drives. These are not usually sold to our friends and family. We freely give our likeness to those we love. This is not the case when it comes to the likenesses of celebrities. Impressions of Britney Spears are made and rapidly reproduced in order to be sold. It would be a mistake, however, to think the only difference between impressions of us and impressions of Britney came because we do not intend ours to be sold. While this is a difference, I think we might do well to also point out there is an aesthetic difference as well. Our likenesses are often candid – fingers in nostrils, goofy looks, captured feeling. Even when we pose for the camera, there is a candid nature because of the fact that it is an event made authentic by the context of our own lives and memories. This is what we might call a *vernacular aesthetic* – an artistic sensibility that is rooted in the realness of living. This aesthetic sharply contrasts with the one employed by Britney and her photographer. Her likeness is predetermined by reproduction. Which is to say her posing is a part of a larger process of capital, selling and purchasing. As such, the posing and airbrushing that occurs in her likeness-taking is at the very best inauthentic, and at the worst completely fake. The contours of her skin, the colour of her hair, the texture of her clothing, are all part of a programme meant for something else besides simple memory. This is the *capital aesthetic*, Britney's aesthetic.

And so, if the base aesthetic movement of her pictures is essentially different from ours, then the result of such image-making art differs as well. Our pictures carry us on into the worlds of our families and friends. I glance at a black and white photograph of my grandparents taken in the 1950s. Although their bodies are no longer with me in a physical sense, their likeness, because of that picture, remains solid in my life. They are present. The photographs of Britney in magazines and on the Internet are not at all present in this way. And perhaps the reason for this lies in the fact that when her picture is taken and reproduced by the millions, so to is her essence disseminated. Consider this: commercial photography might be seen as a tool of capitalism that chips away at the essence of its subjects. I'm not certain this is always the case. For example in the latter half of the nineteenth century, freaks in the New York Bowery had their pictures taken by photographers like Charles Eisenmann. They would take multiple images with Eisenmann, reproduce them by the hundreds, and make a fortune while doing so. All the vendors of the dime Museum circuit, all the rubes in the streets, would pay decent money for a likeness of a fat lady, a Siamese twin, a bearded lady, a midget. These pictures are all about being present. No one would buy a picture of a freak if that freak did not seem active in the frame, available for the onlooker's gaze.[4]

Certainly Britney is available, but she is not there. Pick any of the photographs and ask yourself whether or not you feel the presence of the subject Britney Spears? What we see on the cover, the website, the CD case is a construction of likeness, a manufactured memory, a ghost. She is the freak, but not in the sense of the fat lady, the bearded lady or the midget. Instead, she is what Robert Bogdan refers to as the fake freak, those individuals who feigned physical or mental impairment in order to gain the status of the freak.[5] The only difference with Britney is that she feigned physical perfection. The mental impairment would come later.

And so something happens to Britney during the process of making merchandise. Part of it has to do with the likeness-taking, another part wrapped up in reproduction. Bit by bit, small pieces made from the larger one. Which brings us to the doll.

The Britney Spears fashion doll was released in 1999 by a company called Play Along Toys. While there were other dolls of Britney produced, it is this doll that had the longest run. Like most dolls fashioned after celebrities, the package came with a variety of triggers, in other words pictorial evidence of who the doll was supposed to represent – pictures of Britney performing on stage, a DVD of her music videos, stickers, etc. The clothing matched the clothing from real life, just (barely) smaller.

Smaller is the key word here. Miniaturization as a concept is one with a very rich harvest. The picking apart of Britney via likeness, reproduction and dissemination of photography is superficially quite understandable I think. She is partitioned, split up into many different likenesses that are attached to key chains, buttons, bumper stickers and the like. As a person she is thus chipped down into smaller more purchasable pieces. This miniaturization process, this *dolling down* so to speak, offers a new line of thinking with regards to the issue of merchandising a body. Taken on two levels, miniaturization offers us an insight into the ideas of possession and being. The former seems quite obvious. Owning a doll of Britney Spears has some connection to owning her. All of this happens in the land of play of course, but let's not be too distracted by that. What happens in play? Realities are remade, fantasies are acted upon, laws of experience are rewritten. And so, Britney the doll can perform on the cardboard stage, can help little girls pick out clothing, can encourage the lonely eleven year old, can make cakes in the kitchen, can do the splits, can be stripped naked and ripped apart.

The common argument, first forwarded by people who criticized the Barbie doll in the 1980s, is that the Britney Spears doll had an unconscious, negative impact on these little girls. A healthy body image is unattainable when you compare yourself to plastic, especially molded plastic boobs, buttocks and face. This is a legitimate fear. But it is also one that takes a lazy route, especially when it comes to the empowerment of young women, or at least the offering of empowerment. Certainly a majority of the young women who bought the Britney doll did so because they idolized her, wanted to be her. I suppose some were given the doll by mothers who wanted to be Britney. Either way the assumption of the critics is that these dolls were allowed entrance into the vulnerable psychology of adolescent girls. While I can accept this, it's hard for me to concede that all of them felt bad about themselves when they looked at little Britney. Some did, for sure, but probably not most. Most played with the thing for a week, then left it on the pile in the corner. Most had fun with it, good fun. But then I am sure things went bad for little Britney. She probably got run over by a little brother's army truck, got chewed up and spit out by the dog, got dressed up in all sorts of outfits, had her hair cut way too short by an arts and crafts scissors. In other words, she got worked on – you know she did. And this working on, this mutilation, this fun, is evidence of an empowerment that we rarely give little girls. The Britney doll was fun, but only defined by the little girl herself. This is the essence of possession, isn't it? To own something is to control it. Possession can be fun, because possession itself is something we take pleasure in.

And by being little Britney, possessed by the little girls, the big Britney of real life was also innately becoming a possession. Or at least we can speculate that the little girls who owned little Britney were learning a new lesson of possession. Again, this can go both ways. The critics can say that they were learning about how to become possessions themselves. Or, we could also say that they were learning the adverse effects of objectification. What if a guy, somewhere down the road, took possession of them the same way they took possession of little Britney? That's a pretty clear lesson. Chopped locks of hair, weird outfits, and the inside of a dog's mouth. No thinking needed, they would run for the hills when the jocks called for a date.

But miniaturization has more to do with simply becoming possession. It has to do with *being* itself, with the altered state of existence that comes along with being shrunken. We need to work with the idea forwarded by feminist thinkers that size matters. More particularly, that there has been a discourse about shapes and sizes of women that correlates directly with their position in culture itself. For example, consider the idea of space itself as symbolic. After the rise of feminist movements in the Western world, the space for women grew both philosophically and economically. Put simply, there was just more room for women in the world. However, as we historically moved away from that initial moment of victory, the mediated images of women shrank them back down to a size more manipulatable. So as women gained space in the real world, they lost it in the worlds of imagination. Follow the work of Gloria Steinem to map this out.[6] She realized with her magazine that she had a place in which to allow women more space, much more than pornography or even mainstream movies. Steinem proved that becoming small again, even in the image alone, was unacceptable.

The amount of room available for the experience of women is at stake within the doll. As little Britney looks outside of her cardboard box, stuck on the shelf at some Kmart, what is she thinking? Take me home, get me out of this box, show me your world. Flash forward eight years – wouldn't the big Britney want the same things?

Little Britney was small. And while her (big Britney's) managers put her across as a girl finding her strength, they could not have been clueless of the fact that she was shrinking right in front of their eyes. And so we take miniaturization as a useful social metaphor for the shrinking of women in the cultural sphere. The Britney doll, ironically, becomes something much larger in our understanding of the consumption of Britney Spears. Little Britney becomes the actual Britney by some weird osmosis made possible by capitalism. If we agree that we can buy and sell each other, and call it a part of capitalism, then why might it be so hard to understand little Britney as being Britney herself? Is the manipulation done by the little girl in her backyard any different from anyone else's manipulations of the real Britney? Don't get bogged down with the details, with the absurdity of the idea – instead, let it linger. When we turn on MTV, watch the movie of the week in the theatre, buy MP3s, surf the web, buy the magazine, aren't we all just playing with dolls?

But again, what really is play all about? Manipulation. Violence. New reality.

Notes

1. Steven Johnson, *Everything Bad is Good for You: How Today's Popular Culture is Actually Making us Smarter*. London: Penguin Books, 2005, pp. 3–10.
2. For documentation of the extraordinary commercial success of the rock band Kiss see C.K. Lendt, *Kiss and Sell: The Making of a Supergroup*. New York: Billboard Books, 1997.
3. For more on Weber's understanding of heroism and power, see Max Weber, *From Max Weber: Essays in Sociology*, Hans Heinrich Gerth and C. Wright Mills, eds. London: Routledge, 1998, pp. 248–250.
4. Charles Eisenman was able to capture and represent his freak subjects in a much more active fashion then could his contemporaries. He was able to do this because he employed what I have called a 'collaborative aesthetic'. For more on this argument see Christopher Smit, 'A Collaborative Aesthetic: Lévinas' Idea of Responsibility and the Photographs of Charles Eisenmann and the Late 19th Century Freak-Performer'. In Marlena Tromp, ed., *Victorian Freaks*. Columbus: Ohio State University Press, 2008, pp. 283–311.
5. Robert Bogdan, *Freak Show: Presenting Human Oddities for Amusement and Profit*. Chicago: University of Chicago Press, 1990, p. 8.
6. See Gloria Steinem, *Outrageous Acts and Everyday Rebellions*. New York: Henry Holt & Co., 1995.

Chapter 9

Snakes

On 6 September 2001 at the Metropolitan Opera House in New York City, fans of Britney Spears were teleported first to the nineteenth century, and then to the beginning of it all. Of course, they didn't notice the years slipping past them, the culture slipping away, the taste and brutality slipping downward. Instead, they, along with millions tuned in to the MTV Video Music Awards, witness Britney and a host of other exotics dance to her new single 'I'm a Slave 4U'. The stage is filled with smoke, flashing spotlights, cages with live animals, dancers dressed like tribesmen, female dancers adorned with feathers and face paint. Britney herself is adorned with a tight green bustier; leaves woven into the fabric of her clothing bring to mind images of Eve in the Garden. She is sweaty. The music is tribal – heavy bass brings the rhythm to the top of the throat of the listener. And of course there is the snake. The snake who tempts Eve, who dazzles us, who drapes the slender shoulders of its prey.

All pop culture artifacts have embedded in them these sorts of teleportation devices – let's call them *memory triggers*. Rather than personal memories, or individualized references, most of what is seen and heard in pop culture points toward a sort of cultural, mythical memory, a corner of the cultural imaginary. For example, when we watch the film *Star Wars*, the battle between good and evil that plays out in the galaxy far, far away isn't actually all that far from what we understand through our own history. Through our own understanding of mythology, ethics, Western movies and the like, we know the film before we even see it. Lucas knew this. He knew that we would understand Darth Vader and Luke Skywalker if they were nestled between our memory of conflict and resolution, real or otherwise. Indeed, this is how most popular art works. Dazzle us with contemporary spectacle yet at the same time catch us with a left hook from something we've already seen, felt, done. Go through the following ritual next time you are in the theatre, at a rock concert or reading a novel: trace the storyline backward instead of forward. Don't let the narrative grab you and pressure you into a world where you think that you are bathed in newness. Instead, think about where it, the story, comes from. Think about where you felt the themes before. Follow the cannibalism of the text. Listen to the radio, especially pop radio, and the ritual gets much easier. Follow the drum fills, the guitar licks, the vocal lines, sometimes even lyrics. They are bought and sold like crops. Harvested, consumed, reused.

What makes this work more complex is when the text, or performance, conjures up references within the space of ignorance. Put plainly, when the memory triggers are accidental the text itself becomes paradoxically deeper than its makers could have ever imagined. And by deeper I do not mean better – this is not a sort of surprise value system placed upon the apparently mundane. No, the depth that I am speaking of is much more tragic. This kind of depth shows itself by exposing its own portal of disappointment. This kind of depth is manufactured by happenstance, by good intentions, by the beast of celebrity production. As such it is an unknown by-product that must be known. An unplanned, maybe even unwanted, revelation.

Britney's performance of 'I'm a Slave 4U' in 2001 became a text crammed full of unknown messages. Some of them are on the surface, right there to be seen and heard. Take a minute and find a website with the lyrics to the song.

Let's pay attention to the first 76 words. For even the most casual audience member – the tuned in yet not tuned in video watcher or radio listener – it is quite easy to notice the proclamation being made. She was once something, now she is something else. And that something else is owned by her. Of course we know that she owns nothing of her image by this time, but still we take the bait. She has moved on from the puberty of her career and is now moving into a very real adolescence, a real womanhood. Ironically, the second release from this record would find her saying that she is no longer a girl but yet still not a woman either. Confusion? Desperation? Probably a little bit of both. But in this lyric she is neither confused or desperate – she is powerful, or at least performing power. Note what she is admitting to in the lyric. First, to her age – she is realistic about the fact that she is still young. But instead of embracing this youthfulness, she wants to deny it. She wants to shed the pigtails and replace them with bleached blonde highlights. Second, she wants to admit to feelings, and more particularly desires. Again this is a confession that only makes sense through the context of her early career as a young girl. A third admission, perhaps the most important one, comes in her awareness of being watched, of being the object. She sings with some anger and disappointment about being looked at a particular way. If you listen carefully you might even hear her being fed up with being looked at in any way. To be the object of a glance has certainly sunk in by this point in her career. Videos, interviews, musical performances, etc. have done their jobs.

So what's the hidden message, the reference point that we should see and hear in the lyric? It's quite simple really. This is a new Britney, the first-name only Britney, the title of her new record *Britney*. Britney Spears has grown up. Sex is a part, if not *the* part, of the new woman blazing through the MTV performance. But is this message really hidden? On one hand, the message of sexy Britney gets a little more complex because we know from where she has come. We start playing the comparison game – Mouseketeer Britney versus sexy Britney, *Star Search* Britney versus physical Britney. This creates the 'wow' of the record, the video and the MTV performance of 'I'm a Slave 4U'. And because it does this, because it constructs the spectacle so completely, we must admit that the hidden message is not very hidden at all. In fact it is constructed, just like the lyrics, by people other than Britney herself. So the admissions she makes are made through an interpreter. The yearning she does is only part of an artifice crafted by someone else's yearning for cash. This bites the hardest when we think of the lines about being sick and tired of being watched, being looked at. These words fall flaccid when they are written not by the object but by the looker himself. Think of the twisted logic here. From the mouth of Britney comes a lament, maybe even from the brain of Britney. But the words are false for her, the sentiment is sugar-free. They are fed to her, regurgitated for us, consumed by us. If she really sang these words as a product of her own volition, there would be no video. There would be no performance – there would be no snake.

The marketing of a body is an odd thing, no matter how we have normalized it as a society. The taking and shaping of a soul, of a person, causes their destruction. And it is for this very reason that the song's evocation of slavery marks the trigger of meaning so succinctly. Here is the hidden message that we fail to actually dwell on, even though it's there plain as day. In the context of the song itself, the slavery appears to be to dance music, to rhythm, perhaps to a boy. But this is just too easy to swallow, too easy to pass up a more damaging interpretation. Britney is a slave to so much by this point. Her shackles are forged by her industry, her corporation, her family and her fans. The difference between her and the slaves from our own history is of course wrapped up in the issues of choice and compensation.[1]

Start with this question; did Britney choose to be on the cultural stage? Did she select her own path? Is there anything in the trajectory of her career that balanced on her saying 'Yes, this looks good to me'? Certainly it is difficult for us to answer these questions with precision. But I think we can speculate about whether or not we view the career and life of Britney Spears as something owned by her. As a child she could sing well. But did she want to sing all the time? More to the point, what child can resist the attention, and thus encouragement, of authority figures? And it is easy to see how hours and hours of encouragement and attention can turn into advice, counsel and force. There is no easy way to say this: it is certainly possible that Britney Spears, like any child prodigy, was bullied onto the stage. And if this is true, then the question of choice is answered – there was no choice for an eight year old with cute hair and a good voice. There was no choice for the Mouseketeer to be anything but. There was no choice to record a CD, to perform in a video, to market herself as the All-American southern girl. This is where choice becomes responsibility. Where the decisions are made for you not only by the people who 'run the business' but also by the feeling you get in the pit of your stomach called guilt. If I don't do this to dance, the people who have 'helped' me get here will not get paid. If I don't sing this song that particular way mom and dad won't be able to pay the mortgage. If I am not her, who will I be?

But compensation helps a great deal here. The cool cradle of cash rocks the slave to sleep. In fact we might see the enormous amount of money made by Britney as being a sort of constant lullaby, one that entrances her moment by moment. And in this sense she is no different from any other young celebrity, or old for that matter. Money makes you do crazy things, purchase silly stuff, swallow really sharp realities. It is the great destroyer of inhibition. And often, the killer of innovation. The Beatles are one of the few examples of where wealth reformulated itself into something deserving of our attention and praise. Their last four records were perhaps their best, and they did it all on the back of the compensation they were given during their time of cultural slavery.

We could argue, consequently, that the employment of the idea of slavery by Britney cheapens the sentiment itself. That even though she may have been pushed into a lifestyle that she may or may not have been hesitant about, she has been offered millions of reasons to forget such a beginning. She has been offered so much more than any slave has ever been – food, money, land, opportunity, mobility. And while she has never been offered authentic identity, which she does share with the historic slave, she does retain the gift of white, rich America, that of being culturally flexible. She can be the hero, the druggie, the sex symbol, the bitch, the mother, the star. The slave was and always is the slave. Skin colour, scars and suspicion, these were the clothes of the slave, their birthmark. They were not human. They were animal. Freed only from the pleasures of conscience, morals and ingenuity. What they were left with was instinct. That's all they were given.

Britney's producers play with these images of course, with these impressions of animalistic quality. Watch the performance again and see the presence of *animal*. The caged beast that dances with the savage. Nineteenth-century French anthropologists were instructed by their money men, their armchair anthropologist sugar daddies, to search the world for difference.[2] Their journey was one of inspection and investigation into the dark corners of aboriginal and tribal life. Illuminated by the flashlights of European superiority, these corners of the world offered a wide variety of people, sort of. They weren't people in the sense Matthew Arnold wrote about in *Culture and Anarchy*.[3] First published in 1869, Arnold's essay reads like a manifesto for uplift, a blueprint of what it meant to be a true human being. Essentially his work splits human experience into two categories, that of culture and non-culture. For Arnold, and so many white Europeans from his day, culture represented intellect, beauty and purity. It is here in history where we get the true human journey galvanized – the goal for every man was to be cultured, organized and stately. Those who could not live up to this journey travelled into the land of the savage. The Savage was Other, and to be Other was to be sought out, studied and measured by the skeleton rulers of phrenology.

So with Arnold's cultural project tucked deep inside their khaki pockets, French anthropologists went looking for what they were not. And when they found them, these people/animals, it wasn't enough to study them in their native land. Bodies were exhumed from tribal burial grounds, boiled until any sign of flesh was gone and until the whites of the bone became useful for the scientist. These bones were shipped back to the motherland where they could be studied more completely. The real prize was to actually catch some of these folks, trick them into a cage and into a future of exhibition for scientists and anthropologists too embedded in high society to travel the world. So the cages once used to ship exotic animals from Africa to Europe were now used in the same way, just holding different types of animals.

Swimming together in these cages was a cultural and philosophical desolation, a space without a location, in which the occupants of the cage became symbols of a European decadence. What is in the notion that to understand normalcy is to rape difference? The caged animal of difference is completely object, purely matter made useful through the eyes of a looker. To call this abuse is preposterous – this is colonial corruption made worse by the presence of physical and emotional violence. This is the exotic, man-made. The same spectacle that fuelled the freak show, the sideshow and the dime Museum is easily handed off to the exotic caged animals first witnessed and studied in laboratories but quickly ushered into the halls of a world's fair. What is it like to look out from the cage? Switch your vantage point, cast off your looking position and imagine the madness of being the animal in the cage. Sure, you've paid your dime, you've bought your ticket, you paid for cable and MTV – you deserve this. Or do we?

So the backdrop of Britney's performance of 'I'm a Slave 4U' is made of metal, costumes, make-up, sexy bodies, lights and fake fog. But it is made of so much more. It is made out of a cacophony of cultural and historical tragedy. As a context for this young woman's life, and art, this exotic and animalistic environment screams an unknown naturalism. And yet naturalism can be such a frail and misleading concept. For what is being sold as natural in this performance is not purely an unknown state of being. It is a constructed, deliberate employment of the natural wildness of sex and danger. It is the manipulation of imminent invasion played out on a stage of metaphors and memory triggers. She is the beast, she is the exhibit shipped from the south into the cultural cage of West Coast Hollywood. In this way she is more like the slave than ever. Taken from home, ripped from the everyday and hurled into a horrible newness consisting of work, representation and degradation.

And this snake draped over her shoulders brings it all together. Just like we have noticed the layered usefulness of slavery in understanding and articulating this song and performance, so, too, with the snake. In fact the snake itself is perhaps one of the most overused memory triggers in pop culture today. From the tattooed arms of victims and victimizers on *Law and Order*, to any personification of evil in children's books, the snake conjures an immediate understanding. Evil, primal nature, pain, slick trickery, dangerous, smart, witty and loathsome – all are left behind when the snake strikes. Yet these immediate negative connotations don't seem to help understand why the snake is present on Britney's shoulders. At least no interesting understanding. On a less interesting level the snake is present to play with ideas of the forbidden, of the mystical. See how this works when you picture Britney as the snake charmer. She controls evil, she controls the uncontrollable spirit of the large boa constrictor that caresses her back now rather than attacking it. The lyrics match this, and on a surface level justify the presence of a controllable beast. She controls the snake as she now controls her own life. This is of course an inside looking out interpretation, one desired by Britney's keepers.

But from the outside looking in, with the assistance of history and memory, the snake stands for so much more. It operates as a clue to what lies just underneath the surface of reality being performed in front of our eyes. The snake is the eternal symbol of original sin. Go back to the Garden, watch her grasp the fruit, watch the promise being made by the protective God. Watch the deception of the serpent. Subtract the morality from this sort of connection and understand the symbolic weight of the snake.[4] This is not about Britney stepping away from Christian roots, stepping away from purity, stepping away from God. At least not completely. This is a return to a sort of natural, again naturally constructed, primitive living. God has nothing to do with it, the snake does. Not the snake as Devil, that would be again to moralistic, too simple. The snake here represents a shift back to something that smells like the Earth's core. Gone are the pink ribbons, gone is the edifice of teenager culture, gone is Britney Spears. She is stepping back to something much more primal, much more physical. She, like the snake, is instinctual. She, like the snake, is smooth. She, like the snake, can kill with one bite.

There is a sort of violence here, one justified by years of oppression and manipulation. But again, it is constructed for her not by her. The violence of the snake stands at odds with the violence of production and consumption. Still, it offers a context of violence nonetheless. She is angry, she is animal, she is slave, she is violent. And we've loved it. In other words, our love for the snake in Britney has acted as a solvent for the sting of the bite. We are the taxidermist, stuffing the snake to make it more tangible, more appropriate, more manageable. In the end, the performance on MTV with the snake is a tryout. Watch as she tries out a new dangerous side, a new sexual side steeped in forbidden dance, forbidden movement, forbidden confidence. Once again we tame, we control, we keep her where we want her. It is our violence that we should remember. Ours is the violence that has remained constant from that day in 2001 to today.

Notes

1. Of all the analogies I make in this book, it is this one to slavery that I am most uneasy about. While I do think that the career of Britney Spears illustrates what we might refer to as a stealing of volition, it certainly is not the type of theft witnessed in the history of slavery in the United States. Consequently, allusions I make to slavery should not conjure any specificity for the reader. In other words, I challenge you to evaluate my use of the word slavery based on the merits of my argument here only.
2. For a more complete analysis of nineteenth-century French anthropology and its fascination with the different, spectacular body, please see George W. Stocking Junior, *Race, Culture, Evolution: Essays in the History of Anthropology*. Chicago: University of Chicago Press, 1982, pp. 13–41.
3. Matthew Arnold, *Culture and Anarchy: An Essay in Political and Social Philosophy*. New York: The Macmillan Co., 1920, pp. 31–38.
4. Genesis 3; New International Version.

Chapter 10

The Ease of Digestion

The dynamism of our consumption of Britney Spears is only matched by the ease with which it happened. There are certain things that our bodies do that are effortless to the point of not even knowing it's going on. Like sunburns, sweating or salivating, these mindless motions of physiological and physical happenings go unchecked by our conscious attention. We really only contemplate these things when something goes wrong. Focus on the sunburn for just one second. Think about the effortless Sunday afternoon on the beach. What gets our focus, what earns our monitoring on such a day are things like picnic food, cold beer, bodies in swimsuits and maybe a baseball game on a radio. The breeze from the ocean embraces us in such a way that we are lost in its gentility. We are seduced by the odours of the beach, the coconut oil worn by our lover, the faint whisper of barbecue, the scent of gasoline from a nearby fishing boat. It is only as we drive home that we begin to sense the tightening of our skin, the strains of our sunburned flesh, that something has gone awry. The casualty of our effortless enterprise is blistered skin, soon to be flaky remnants of a day spent in the sun.

If we were to think about popular culture reception and consumption as a sort of physiological and even physical event, the following revelations might occur: the makers of the pop world, both artists and producers, need us to be in a very comfortable, effortless state while consuming their product. They want the digestion to go smoothly. They want it to be effortless, invisible. And we comply, dancing with them through learned routines. The invisibility of this event is at the very core of what we might call the *popular aesthetic*, a seemingly natural design and execution of art and its audience. In Film Studies, scholars refer to the classic Hollywood narrative as one of these invisible dances.[1] A film begins by clearly identifying the players – the protagonist wearing white, the antagonist wearing black, the buddies, the cohorts, the funny, chubby guy, the trophy blonde, the sidekick, the scapegoat. Once we know who these people are, and exactly how they will act, the film conflict arises. Somebody needs the money, someone needs to die in order for the other to live, somebody can't be themselves unless something else happens. Most of the film follows our players struggling with this conflict which eventually hits a climactic moment which finds them acting at their best, most heroic state. And then of course there is the resolution. The happy ending where every element of the conflict is subsided, where every character reaches their pinnacle of personhood, where we can all breathe a sigh of relief.

Good films, or so the theory goes, mess around with this classic dance just enough to keep us on the edge of our seats. For example, if a film's resolution is sad, tragic or even violent, we are fooled into believing that this is something new, something we've never seen before. But if we really reflect on it we might admit to ourselves that even though things seem alternative, they are simply the result of shifted playing pieces in the same puzzle we have broken down and put together on every Christmas Eve since we were four years old. This is not to say that there are no pieces of art in the popular world that reject the formulaic nature of its context. Rather, what we need to realize is that there is a sort of formula that no popular art can leave behind. Even the best art is reactionary. And really, we don't want it any other way. Since the end of the war to end all wars, our consumption of popular art has always been done after work, after we have earned our keep in the factory of our jobs. Leisure time, an invention of booming postwar economy, is itself a sort of formula. We do our thinking at work and we do our playing in the theatres, concert halls and gin joints of our towns. When we consume, in other words, we are usually exhausted. Or caught up in something else. Thus, consumption has been cheapened into a state of being.

What has made this so complex over the last 30 years or so is that our leisure time has gained more importance than our work. I see this most clearly in the context of my work as a professor. My college students have widescreen TVs, the best digital technology available for their music collection and so forth. Prices go down as these gadgets accumulate cultural capital, or so the big business would have us believe. In all actuality prices have gone up alongside our willingness to spend. When Apple released its new phone my students lined up in the mall to get one, about $450. Some of them work for this money, no doubt. But others? It's those others that make me pause. Consumption is breathing for them, for us. That state of being that seems naturalized by companies like Apple, IBM and McDonald's.

Consumption and spending are invisibly connected in the womb of contemporary experience. In fact we might begin to realize that our spending is in itself a consumable product, a phenomenon that occurs in the same invisible space occupied by the sunburned beachgoer. This morning I was paid electronically by my college, a non-event that happens twice a month without me even acknowledging it. Alongside the deposit into my checking account comes automatic withdrawals, money sifting through the cyberspace without effort. And so while I gather some coin I immediately dispense of it, or put more succinctly, my avatar does. As I have my morning cigarette on my deck with my dogs I have given out roughly $1,000 to computers across the country. Mine is just one example of the manner in which capital leaves us effortlessly, without any contemplation. And is this any different from the family who visits the outlet mall? Everyone tumbles out of the minivan at 10am, plans to meet at the food court at 1pm are made, and within that three hours hundreds of dollars can be spent without even seeing it leave their wallets: discounted clothing that we don't need, hardware supplies that we cannot live without, and toys and CDs from the bargain bins. The money is ours, but not really. The only thing that we really have is stuff.

Note that this is consumption at its best, especially in the eyes of the popular culture proprietor. This is not, however, digestion. Again, remind yourself that this shopping spree at the outlet mall is done sans pain, sans difficulty, sans anything conscious. It just happens. Digestion of these consumables might happen two, three, four months down the road when the car breaks down and you have no expendable cash to pay for it. It may happen when your son or daughter gets ill and your insurance deductible glares at you unannounced. Here is where digestion actually happens. When we consume in the popular realm we rarely digest – this is especially true in the West. It just goes in, finds its place and settles for the night, the year or the decade, and then leaves us. Digestion takes energy and work. According to doctors, who know much more than I do about how the body works, only about 15 per cent of what we eat is actually absorbed and digested by our bodies. The rest is excreted through urine and faeces. As a metaphor for our consumption of popular product, this can be very illuminating. This can open the eyes of our stomach.

As pointed out earlier, to make consumption work its way into digestion there needs to be some sort of disruption, some sort of wrongness that catches our effort. This is the roughage of Pop life rarely seen or felt. This is the all-bran product that grabs onto electrolytes, polysaccharides and other proteins necessary for real metabolism to occur. Without such disruption all that we take in just turns to waste. And so for real digestion of popular culture there needs to be a momentous event of disturbance, of confusion, of interruption from the routine of reception.[2]

If you take a minute, you may be able to create a list of popular art that asks us to digest, or rather demands us to do some digesting. To help you get started: any film made by Oliver Stone (most are awful, but certainly filled with roughage), the records of Bob Dylan, jazz, some of the films by Michael Moore (I won't tell you which ones), the documentary photography of Dorothea Lange, the art photography of Diane Arbus, the blue series by Pablo Picasso, anything written and recorded by Lucinda Williams and the life and art of Johnny Cash.[3]

The point here, of course, is that Britney Spears remains in the undecided column; we do not know whether to ascribe her with the value of consumable or digestible. Certainly, if you mark her career as I have done above, it seems that both classifications could be assigned. On one hand, she has been purely consumable, as a body, as a voice, as a product of other people's energy. Our energy has not been needed. On the other hand, what we don't recognize is that Britney has been completely digested and worked on. She has been chewed thoroughly, broken down in order to feed the energy source of our collective living. But has this digestion been too easy? We understand that she has been consumed – that seems obvious at this point. But the digestion part is much more sticky, much harder to decipher.

Digestion metaphors are many, certainly too many to summarize here. The Romantics used them to understand and employ the idea of love, the Greeks used them to contemplate spirituality, and so forth. Practices of Western religion give us the most applicable metaphors through which to understand Britney. In 1549, the following prayer was included in the first English prayer book:

> Blessed Lord, who hast caused all holy Scriptures to be written for our learning; Grant that we may in such ways hear them, read, mark, learn, and inwardly digest them, that by patience, and comfort of thy holy Word, we may embrace, and ever hold fast the blessed hope of everlasting life, which thou hast given us in our Savior Jesus Christ.

Such a grand and swooping sentiment may at first seem out of place when contemplating a pop star. However, drawing parallels between digesting scripture and digesting Britney Spears may be just the shock we need to begin reimagining our consumption. It is therefore within the absurd that we might figure out absurdity itself – another metaphor for understanding Pop life. Ponder the usefulness of the second line of this prayer, where the person on one knee asks that they may inwardly digest the word of God. Such a proposition, such a request demands that consumption requires a sort of permission, that the devout reader of the word needs to be guided in her understanding by something outside of him or herself. This should itself be an indicator of what 'good' digestion is really all about – asking, receiving and thanking.

Thus, our consumption of Britney is not only mindless and effortless – it is also, again, a sort of violence. In other words, we are not given permission by the woman herself to take part in her life, to play a role in her creation. Capitalism has created a new sort of permission, one in which we feel entitled to 'it' because we have paid for it. And isn't our money simply another representation of us, our hard work, our toil, our lives? So because we give up our selves, our capital, we assume a sort of authority, a sort of false aristocracy over the lowly stars and celebrities that entertain us. To call this violence is not pushing too far, especially if we define violence as actions taken without permission. And yet it is a sort of passive violence, effortless because we do not recognize our own exertion of control. Instead, we think we have control over the equilibrium in our lives, our ability to work, purchase and consume. But alongside the everydayness of control is the cumulative effect, a damaging invasion into the lives of those we purchase.

Some may argue that we are given permission by Britney to control her. Certainly she gains a good deal by our purchasing, devotion and attention. And she does play the part – she is the star, the rock queen, the one in the music videos, on the stage, on the CD. Isn't she to blame for her own abuse? While I am rationally capable of understanding this line of argument, my soulful reaction is completely the opposite. I have chosen to look at this woman through the eyes of oppression, injustice and violence. You may choose otherwise, but you should ask yourselves why. Why is it that we want Britney to be complicit with her own downfall? Why do we need Britney to be a part of the equation of violence that we have outlined above? Again, I think the answer to these and questions like them have to do with permission. We need permission to keep feeling okay.

Take away permission and the story of the consumption of Britney Spears grows dark. Moreover, take away a desire for permission and see what happens: the creation of a situation in which it doesn't matter whether or not she deserves what she has been given. Take away permission and lose the veil of authority, of a good time. Take away permission and watch as we finally begin to understand the implications of our actions. I know this seems one-sided, that our consumption of Britney is allour fault. And maybe it's not. But unless we see it this way at least once, we cannot truly digest us and her. We need to finish our meal. We need to do new work.

We need to do so because in the prayer, the step which follows permission is acceptance. Acceptance of the fact that we need to be patient in order to be hopeful, that we need to be listeners instead of talkers, aware instead of voyeuristic, people of protection rather than procrastination, of integrity rather than isolation. The whole problem of our consumption of Britney Spears is grounded in the fact that we have not digested the realization that she needed us as much as we thought we needed her. And her need goes way beyond money, power, spectacle, sex, love and devotion. No, the need I am speaking here is one for community, respect and protection. This is neither maternal or paternal – she's had enough of that sort of attention. This need arises from communal interaction the likes of which we rarely see.

Unfortunately, this need never made it to the surface of our stomachs, we never grew up or threw up the right stuff in order to learn. Instead we turned our heads and ate some more.

Notes

1. David Bordwell, Janet Staiger and Kristin Thompson, *The Classical Hollywood Cinema: Film Style & Mode of Production to 1960*. London: Routledge, 1985, pp. 2–41
2. Movies about the life of Jesus are great vehicles for these sorts of moments. Paul Schrader's *The Last Temptation of Christ* (1988) and Mel Gibson's *The Passion of the Christ* (2004) serve as great examples to briefly place flesh on the metaphor. Both films deal with a character deeply embedded within the experiences and imaginations of audiences. The former challenges while the latter blatantly affirms this man Jesus and his work. Schrader, who attended a Christian college in the 1970s, uses his film to suggest an alternative reality for the carpenter from Galilee, one in which he (the filmmaker) seeks to know how doubt and temptation might have worked in the life of so many people's Messiah. The disruption thus comes towards the climax of the film when Jesus, while hanging on the cross, daydreams one final daydream about giving in to worldly temptation and sleeping with Mary Magdalene. When he awakes, he awakes for all, and takes on the burden of being the Christ. This disruption in the historic narrative of Jesus acted as a puncture in the expectation of the Christian viewer. It asked them to not only consume but digest the message of the film – to use energy and effort in their perception. Gibson offers this disruption as well, but in a way not so expected. In one of the most violent films of the last ten years, Gibson portrays with minute detail the flagellation of Jesus. With bones and blood and flesh, Gibson puts in visual image what the Gospels had only attempted before. Here there is affirmation of the sacrifice made by Jesus in a spectacular and grotesque form. Again, the audience is disrupted by the image they are made to digest.
3. Tread lightly when you create your own list of disruptive art, for you can easily run into the slippery slope of elitism. This is what my students tell me constantly as I destroy their taste for Sylvester Stallone, Johnny Depp, popular fiction and radio rock. Some of you may be fine with being elitist. If you can defend it, go for it. However, do not take my list or your list as the definitive account of what matters in the world of art, popular or otherwise. If you do you'll risk missing the enjoyment of a mindless comedy, a feel-good flick where everybody falls in love, blaring songs by Toto, Kelly Clarkson and REO Speedwagon on the way to a summer party. Some things are not meant to be digested. Some things are glorious speed bumps on our way to someplace else.

Part III

Exile

Chapter 11

Exile on Main Street

You will leave everything you love most:
this is the arrow that the bow of exile
shoots first. You will know how salty
another's bread tastes and how hard it
is to ascend and descend
another's stairs ...

Dante[1]

The difficulty of understanding the space which Britney Spears inhabited during her exile does not concern volition, blame or justification. Instead, the problem stems from language, and a lack of it. We don't have a word or concept that neatly encompasses what has happened to this woman. *Rolling Stone*'s use of the word 'tragedy' helped our articulation, but only slightly.[2] The image of tragedy that most of us have is one garnered by spectatorship – we *know* tragedy because we have *watched* tragedy. And when something tragic happens in our own life, it is an odd thing to actually label it as such, as something occurring in real time. When a family member dies, for example, these tragic events become something much different. They become conspicuous reality, not tragic. It takes somebody else to label it that. Vanessa Grigoriadis, the author of the article for *Rolling Stone*, modified tragedy with the label 'American'. This label seems even less illuminating. What is American about Britney's tragedy? Is there a sort of pattern of perpetuating pop decay in the United States? Maybe – but the author never answers this question in her article. Instead, she leaves us compiling lists of American tragedies in which we might categorize Britney. Assassinations of presidents, wrongful wartime action, acts of violence, environmental chaos and the fall of a pop star. Doesn't the latter seem out of place?

It is odd that we must find a new language for something we have done, something we have initiated, over and over again. Moreover, something that we have done without much effort. The fall of Britney Spears has occurred in front of us, behind us and right in the middle of us – it has been a ubiquitous event. Nonetheless, many of us have been spectorally implicated at the very most, innocent bystanders at the very least. And what we have watched can be named by many words that may at first glance seem to be preposterously overblown: tragedy, of course, but also destruction, deterioration, gluttonous digestion, violence, rape, annihilation, demolition, obliteration and abandonment. All of these words fit awkwardly because of our distance from the acts themselves. Consider the fact that most of us would say that those things done to Britney were done by others – by media reporters, photographers, paparazzi – by *them*, not us. And yet, if McLuhan is correct, then the media are simply an extension of ourselves.[3] They are connected to the corporeality of our limbs, senses and psyche. The audio of our ears, the video of our eyes, the touch of our technology – our whole being is mediated. If we fashioned this idea to its culmination of a philosophical reality, then we are closer to understanding that what has been done to Britney has been done by us.

And yet those terrible actions listed above still seem distant and hard to accept. Perhaps many of us think that Britney herself was complicit in her own destruction. She is to blame for her public spectacles, parenting debacles and marriages. To let the idea of her own involvement sink in, watch fifteen minutes of her and her then husband Kevin Federline's ridiculous reality show. How absurd, these late-night conversations in the tour bus. Fumbling with words and emotions, a surely drunk Britney is dangling by a thin thread of respect and candour. She is playing the role given to her, certainly, but she is also revelling in it. She signed a contract, she was aware of viewers. So why isn't this destruction her own fault?

It may be partially her fault. I will admit that.

But this admission, this acceptance of complicit behaviour on the part of Britney Spears, cannot be our nexus moment. It cannot be the end of our discussion here. Putting it as plainly as I can: to manufacture a scenario in which victims of cultural punishment are more responsible for their castigation than the victimizer (the culture) is a historical mistake we have too often made. And so to read on in this last section is to admit, or be open to, the following:

> Britney Spears, the pop star, has been *our* creation from the beginning.
> The celebrity of Britney Spears is, in part, *our* responsibility, *our* fault.
> *We* have very little knowledge of who Britney Jean Spears *actually* is.
> *We* have exiled Britney Spears, the pop star.
> *We* have exiled Britney Jean Spears, the woman.
> *We* control her comeback.

Six statements meant to obliterate complacency, to momentarily disentangle us from the media web, to direct us into a new headspace and also to prompt us to employ a new language for an old action. The idea of exile. It works as an umbrella concept, one that envelops the other list of destruction verbs. It gathers them in a concise fashion, one that avoids glossing over, pushing away or dusting under. And it's also a concept, a word, that implicates as much as it explicates. It's a word that is about us as much as it is about her.

(Curious about my use of the identifiers 'us', 'we' and 'our'? Some may be pulling away at this point because they are not a fan of Britney Spears, because they are older than the kids they assume make up her fans. Indeed, some could be wondering about my collective language based on the disagreement they are having with my assumptions about the centrality of the Internet, digital communication and consumption in cultural life. To these concerns I point out the following: if any element of in your life garners meaning from digital, mediated or Internet-based platforms, you are part of the permission given to exile Britney Spears. By participating in the system, you are valuing it. And when we value something, we give it power. Furthermore, this power is global, free of racial, national, gender, class or age specificity.)

Poetic flourishing and grand paintings have cleaned up the notion of exile to make it something at one time desirable. For the Romantics, exile was a state of glory, a place and space one desired to inhabit. Such seclusion would render the poet or the painter disenfranchised from his surroundings, a separation of body and soul that in turn would reconnect him to the contours of his own inner landscape. The destination is the self. In this practice, the artist chooses to be separated from culture. Indeed, separation itself becomes an art form, a palette of time and space. The process of disengagement, something rarely felt these days, offered the vagabond new colours to paint with, new words to speak with, new forms of articulation. Some modern Romantics still do this. Dress yourself in isolation, like Johnny Cash did, and the sensation makes for wonderful music.

But let's not get carried away on the wings of artistic mechanics. The other type of exile, the one most frequently seen in history, is not self-induced.[4] It is not chosen, not desired, not at all glorious. In fact, more traditional social exile operates as a violent dislodging of those individuals felt to be unfit or unworthy of community. The disabled, the sexually different or deviant, the racially mixed, the poor, the criminal, the motherless, the captives, the dreamers, the visionaries, the mangled, the bastards – these were, these are, the exiles. Bending under the will of the many, these passengers of social upheaval operate as symbolic purging, thrown up and left on the ground of what we do not want to look at, to feel, to be. There is a lesson to be learned early on from these exiled: bodies, identities and people are as thinly made as paper trash, all can crumble under the weight of waste.

People have been exiled for religious affiliation, political manoeuvering and expression of social dissatisfaction. In other words, one common justification for exile is belief. Many have been disregarded and sent away because the things that guided their heart and mind fell far from the common imagination that surrounded them.

Others have been exiled because of the very essence of their existence, their state of being. Read ancient Jewish or Christian accounts of exile and see that a common element of those sent away was some physical or mental difference. Communities of skin disease, of blood passions, offer a rare glimpse of what we can call a community of exile. Here we have visions of collectivity among those not collected, an absurd yet completely human community of unwanteds. Nonetheless, difference meant exile. Trace the history of the mentally ill in Europe and the United States, and you will see the same story. Follow with Michel Foucault the timeline of the asylum, the sanitarium, the mad houses of France.[5] These are narratives of exile. If your mind worked differently, if your body was shaped or employed awkwardly, exile was your future.

Furthermore, all exile is symbolic; the exiled body is both symbolically and physically removed from normal community. However, biblical exile, ancient exile of all kinds, often carried with it an additional undertone of sacrifice. The leper is sent away not only because she is contagious, but because she, like no other, can carry the sin of the people to their God. Follow the girl outside of town. Shoulders bent, face hidden, she walks awkwardly outside the gate of the town in which she was born, in which she had a family, in which she had found love. Leaving is permanent, soul-wrecking. The disease that scratches her skin from the bone came to her brother first, then her sister, and they both died. She tried to hide the red marks, but they eventually took over her whole body. She placed pieces of her in the dirt behind her house, hoping that they would regenerate, fix themselves so that she could affix them again. But they failed, God failed. She was made to believe that her broken skin was made so purposefully. Hard to swallow when you can't swallow without pain. Her village, her parents, prayed over her body, and the words soothed at first. But then they changed. How could she carry the sins of all of these people? How could a sickly nineteen-year-old girl bear the weight of a man's adultery, a woman's jealousy, the lust of the town boys, the broken innocence of the town girls? Why did she have to?

And where did she go, where should she go? The gate closes as her exile opens. Like all exiles, the destination is wilderness. The girl with the broken skin stumbles towards the shade of the trees not knowing whether or not she will make it through the night. She craves water, the water her family and town denied her. She craves food, also denied. To meet God, the exile must be in its purest state, broken and empty. But this girl is not empty; she is full of pain, memory and ambition. She is scared, alone. And she stays that way until her death, two days later on a hill. For her there is no Holy respite waiting. When she drew her last breath she did not see God. All she saw was her skin and the wild.

The girl with the broken skin is exiled in order for her people to live. That is why she is exiled. Although reasoning, justification and understanding are hard to grasp in the process of exile, we must ask ourselves if and why Britney has been dealt this fate? How she was exiled will come later. That's a story most of us know. But for now, we must ask why. Was it for a certain belief she held? Was it for the state of her existence, something essential in her being? Was it symbolic? To be more appropriate, these questions of course should be asked in the present tense – her exile is still happening. Even in her comeback, she remains the exiled.

With regards to belief we have a fairly complicated situation to consider. Is there a belief system held by Britney that counters that of the public? Is there reason to believe that she fell short of the cultural imagination surrounding her, especially pertaining to celebrity? I don't think we can answer these questions with a confident 'yes'. In fact, we must admit to the opposite, to the fact that she bought in 100 per cent to the guiding logic about celebrity, fame and most importantly, capitalism. Here is a girl who, for her entire childhood, lived on the lifeblood of a capitalist dream – she knew the by-product of effort, she knew the cost of achievement and, unconsciously, she knew her role as both capital seeker and capital itself. From adolescence to adulthood, her business savvy certainly grew. She was a player in the system that she had created, a manipulator of money and appearance both. Her blood flowed green, just like ours. So her belief system, at least economically speaking, was not alien to her surroundings. Not at all.

And if we were to speak of her religious belief system, as we already have, then again we have to admit that she fits right in. She was created by God to do something special, just like many Americans believe. Even patriotism, a belief now up for grabs in 2010, became part of her belief matrix. Watch her on TV supporting George Bush and his war in Iraq.

Of course these are the beliefs that we see, that we saw, clearly. In terms of her other beliefs about, say, sexuality, family, women's rights, marriage and personal identity, we have no idea. We think we have her number here, but really we don't. All we have is projection, our suspicions placed on her belief. And so still the answer is no, she was not exiled for her belief.

With belief systems not offering much help in our answer, we turn to being, or more specifically, the condition of Britney's body and mind. Start by realizing that the belief systems of capitalism and religion swim their way through Britney's body. Literally speaking, these two ideologies become the canvas on which her body is painted by herself, her mother and her producers. When you understand the cultural or political gains of physical effort, the body becomes much more than a site of living, eating, breathing. The body becomes a portal, a machine designed to achieve more. And in the context of celebrity and Pop life, the body is everything. The body becomes the site wherein most work is done by the celebrity – hairstyle, skin tone, skin health, the colour of teeth, the colour of eyes, the size and shape of all the body parts, especially breasts, stomach, butt, legs and feet. You begin the search for all sorts of products to keep your body in the condition expected of it. Your body is your money.

But the body became much more for Britney Spears. Her body became the emblem of her. It became the one recognizable physical marker of her career, her music, her aspirations. In other words, the body became what Rosemarie Garland Thomson prefers to call 'pure body', a designation she gave to the freak show performers of the nineteenth century.[6] Garland Thomson explains with complexity that freak performers were hardly performers at all. Instead, they were physical examples of difference, purely flesh and spectacle. Several hundred years before she wrote her book, Martin Luther had made similar comments about a young boy with mental retardation.[7] In his story, he recounts meeting a prince on a bridge who had been bothered by the young boy. When his students asked what Luther would have done with the boy, he answered quite simply that he would have thrown the boy into the river to drown. Why? Because the boy was soulless, solely flesh and bone. Britney's body became this, to the tee. A source of capital without a soul, a source of action without consequence, a source of pleasure without pain.

The body of Britney Spears was put high on the mantle, up on the shelf of our aspirations and hopes. It was without exaggeration the perfect body, for men and women. The perfect contours of her skin, the luxurious curves of her body, both entice and inspire. And yet they also angered, frustrated, confused and enraged. Her body is the first site of her exile. When it failed the first time, when it looked larger thanks to pregnancy, when it was pictured grotesquely in the backseat of an SUV, it became real, concrete, living. And this was a letdown for those who waved the banner of Britney's perfection. They felt abandoned, to the point of feeling old and unwanted. This body which had brought so much joy, so much pleasure, was now for the first time giving something else – a mirror, a scary glimpse back at ourselves and our appetites. What we saw was not pretty. Not just her body, which was simply a mature adult body, but the wolf staring back. Our own desire and clenching teeth were too much, and we said goodbye. We banished her, her body, the lust for it.

We would perform the same task for her mind. When the cognitive abilities of Britney Spears slid under the lens of inquiry, of assassination, it too failed. When the body goes, so goes the mind. I spend my days in a wheelchair, so my body looks awkward to others, mostly people who don't know me, who don't know my mind. Those are the folks that assume my physical limitation comes with a mental one as well. I gave a lecture once at a conference, after which somebody came up to me and asked me, very slowly, 'Are you having a good time young man?' I had just spent an hour talking to my audience about how dialogical philosophy helps us read disabled art. And this person, the one now talking slowly to me, was in that audience apparently listening to me speak. I realize now that she was not talking to me at all. She was talking to a representation of me carved out by my body and consequently my mind. When the body fails, our society assumes that the mind is made feeble in order to compensate for the broken expectations of physical exertion. This was the case in the attack on, and subsequent understanding of, the mind of Britney Spears. And so the second site of her exile cycle is her brain.

But exile, in the ancient sense, is to pitch away completely. Exile follows the girl with the broken skin into the wilderness, into the dark emptiness. Alone, in isolation, goes the exile. Contemporary exile works differently. The exile of Britney Spears, initiated on account of her body and mind, did not send her to some expansive place of contemplation. We exiled her to Main Street. We wanted to watch her exiling just as we had watched her creation and consumption.

So the word exile helps us get to one moment of understanding, but it also introduces us to a new one, one fashioned for our particular cultural moment. Contemporary exile is a rehearsal of symbolic ancient exile in that it asks the exiled body to carry with it the sins, transgressions and fears of a culture. The difference happens after the exile begins her walk away. Contemporary culture wants to watch. Contemporary exile will be televised, will fill the screens of our computers, the pages of our magazines. We will take part in the exile. We will be its messenger as well as its chaperone. Is this the goal of contemporary life? To be involved in the destruction and the construction of each other's lives? To be involved, even if by digital manufacturing, in the dark and dirty lives of others. This makes our lives feel more clean. This is the savouring of Pop life for the consumer: what we want, the way we want it and when we want it. Britney was ours when she was up, so much more so when she was down. We paint the good picture and the bad one. And we're getting better at the latter. We were trained by TMZ. Or are they trained by us?

Creeping around bushes, watching from the hilltops, surveying with the mediated telescope, the town watches the woman with the broken skin. We are there when she stumbles in the wilderness. We are there, just out of her sight, when she cries from hunger. We are there when she searches for God, when she slips and falls, when she breaks her skin in anger, when she shaves her head to avoid the heat, when she acts like no one else acts.

Notes

1. Dante, Paradiso XVII: 55–60.
2. See Vanessa Grigoriadis, 'The Tragedy of Britney Spears', *Rolling Stone*, 21 February 2008, http://www.rollingstone.com/news/story/18310562/cover_story_the_tragedy_of_britney_spears.
3. For more on McLuhan's ideas regarding the media as extensions of the human body see Marshall McLuhan, *Understanding Media: The Extensions of Man: Critical Edition*, W. Terrence Gordon, ed. New York: Gingko Press, 2002.
4. The practice of exiling has deep roots in both Jewish and Christian traditions, as well as other religious histories. In order for you to understand my use of the word exile, I will point you to three sources, all of which to a varying degree deal with the practice of exile via the lenses of philosophy, history and poetry: Ovid, *The Poems of Exile*,. Trans. and ed. Peter Green. Los Angeles: University of California Press, 2005; Hannah Arendt, *Essays in Understanding 1930–1954: Formation, Exile, and Totalitarianism*, Jerome Kohn, ed. New York: Schocken Books, 1994; Peter R. Ackroyd, *Exile and Restoration*. Philadelphia: The Westminster Press, 1968.
5. Michel Foucault, *Madness and Civilization: A History of Insanity in the Age of Reason*. Abington: Routledge, 1989.
6. Rosemarie Garland Thomson, *Extraordinary Bodies: Figuring Physical Disability in American Culture and Literature*. New York: Columbia University Press, 1997, p. 64.
7. Martin Luther, *Luther's Works*. St Louis: Concordia Press, 1955–1986, vol. 54: 397.

Chapter 12

Motherhood

We don't want our child celebrities to grow up. When they do, it is so awkward. One example of this that seems so obvious is Danny Bonaduce. The quintessential cute suburban kid playing in a rock 'n roll band with his family the Partridges, Danny was the boy I wanted to be. Rather than doing the mundane routines of my own childhood – going to school, packing a lunch, watching cartoons – I wanted to do what Danny was doing. I wanted to play music with my family. Actually, I wanted to play music with *his* family. My heart and soul longed to go on tour like he did, be on television like he was, hang out with his cute sister. I had two brothers, very boring, very normal. The truth is I had a very musical family, my grandfather for example was a professional drummer. My own immediate family sang all the time, and every Christmas put on a show for churches in the Chicagoland area. Sure, it wasn't rock 'n' roll, but I was on stage. The difference between Danny and me, the Partridges and the Smits, was that we were not televised. We were not in the magazines young teenagers read. We were not famous. We were not paid.

As we grew up, the differences between Danny and me became that much clearer. In fact, thankfully, I began to admire my own existence even more than Danny's. While I was growing up, getting girlfriends, playing in rock bands, Danny went dark. His body morphed in weird ways – muscular, but not in a good way. We never expected him, never wanted him, to change physically. What was really bizarre was that his face, his eyes, his freckles, never changed. Just his body. My memory of him and my awareness of his growing up blended in a way that made him look like a bobble-head doll, like someone stuck the same head on a different torso. A sort of Frankenstein. And this Frankenstein got angry about growing up, took a bunch of drugs, drank a bunch of alcohol, became an addict, became schizophrenic and landed back on television. This time he was himself, his dark self, in a documentary show on VH1. If it is the dream of every child star to return to the cradle of media, which I'm not sure it is, then Danny's dream was becoming a reality. Literally.

It's an awful show. Danny and his wife go to a psychotherapist to get their train wreck of a marriage fixed, he struggles with drugs and sexual addictions, she goes on shopping sprees, and we are there with them. For what reason, I do not know. It's painful to watch. But the pain is not only from the content of the show. The pain is also a product of realizing that this man's life is some sort of nostalgic performance. His *life*, imagine that. Indeed, imagination has everything to do with the pain that has become his life. He is trying to live an imaginary existence, one that formerly brought him pleasure, money and fame. And this is what we want, his audience. We don't want him to grow up and become normal. We don't want the dark Danny, really. I mean, we will take him and revel in his demise, but that's not what we really want. We want him to be who he was. And the problem with this cycle is that he has, like many other child celebrities, internalized our desire. He has become us, his hope has become our hope. We all want to be young again.

This destruction cycle can be repeated over and over, and it has been. In fact, it is this cycle which we find at the heart of our exiling of Britney. But of course, with Britney we make it more complicated, a more sophisticated destruction. Consider how we change the formula for her, and maybe other female child celebrities: things get tricky because we don't want her to mature, but we do want her to become a woman. We want to stunt the growth of her personality, we want her to stay innocent. But we also want her to have the breasts of a woman. We want to sexualize her but we want her to stay a child. This is a common visual theme in pornography and advertising. Note the number of images of women in which they are eroticized by the very act of making them look like little girls.[1] And this doesn't have to be explicit, doesn't have to be marked by the presence of ribbons in pigtails or baby doll dresses. It can be a glance, an expression, a position of childlike innocence. It all boils down to vulnerability: make the woman vulnerable and you will make her innocent; take away her power and she becomes the perfect piece of art.

But is this something that we all wanted from Britney? Did we all want her to be the sexual yet innocent type? Who is encapsulated in my use of the word 'we'? Partitioning the audience of Britney Spears can be dangerous because it allows a certain immunity for given populations of that community. Consequently, my use of the word 'we' tends to be all-encompassing. Because I think even the little girl who loves Britney controls the star, manipulates her. Even those who don't consider themselves fans of Britney get caught up in the digital world that helped create and break her. Not so innocent bystanders. We all manipulate her, just in different ways. But sexualization, especially in the way described above, perhaps stretches the willingness to conglomerate all Britney consumers into one group. By the time Britney's second CD is released it is obvious that sex has become her key aesthetic. How does this work, how is it consumed, by the different demographics of her audience? For the girls her own age it operates as a ruler, a measurement of who they might be if they tried hard enough. Certainly this is the case when you consider the clothing trends

Britney begins in this group of girls – ripped jeans, lacy tops, tight, tight, tight, pants that show off thongs – we have Britney to thank for all of this. For the boys her age, it also became a gauge by which to measure their own desires. In the same way pin-up girls operated for soldiers during World War II, Britney photographs and products tempted young men into believing that all women, even ones they would take out on Friday night, needed to be a particular sexual product.

For the older crowd, specifically heterosexual men and women, the sexual aesthetic of Britney worked differently. For women, I can speculate about at least two responses. One is fear. This too can be bifurcated into several different motivations. For the protective mothers, Britney was everything they didn't want their daughters to become. For other mothers, they feared that Britney was everything their daughters would become if they didn't crack down with rules about clothing, curfews and dating. And still for other mothers, there must have simply been the fear of growing up, and more specifically, a fear about the popular cultured atmosphere that her daughter was growing up in. When sex becomes a key element of the community laying claims on children, parents get nervous. The second fear for adult women might have been generated by simply being older, at least older than Britney. The presence of spectacle, especially one that people eagerly invest in, obliterates the normal. Britney made all hairstyles seem boring, made all bodies seem conspicuously plain.

For heterosexual men, she was a danger. And this too is a multifaceted danger, one we probably can assume to know already. She was a danger because she challenged the sexual attractiveness of their partners, not unlike other popular female celebrities. Note, I am not arguing that all men operate on the level of skin and curves. Not all men find their partners the way popular proprietors want them to. But for the ones that do, Britney must've been a dangerous alternative image for men to employ. She was also dangerous because of the powerful association she created for men when they considered younger women in their own lives. Britney sexualized late twentieth-century teenage girls, there is no doubt of that. This monumentally affects girls, but it also effects the men who gave those girls allowances to buy the CDs, posters and all the other stuff of Britney. Put up a poster Britney in your room, and dad will certainly see it. It might even get stuck in the brain, on his way to work, when he drives past the high school and sees the cheerleader squad practising for the weekend game. He's not perverted, he's just human, making associations.

It should not be assumed that the audiences of Britney Spears are only heterosexual. Doing so ignorantly bypasses the presence of a homosexual market for the star. All the demographics discussed here can be shared by both heterosexual and same-sex attractions. Speculation on my part, a heterosexual male, leads me to think that gay adolescence held a special place for Britney, especially for boys. My gay male students often share with me their fascination with female celebrities. This is especially true with Madonna. As I understand them, their attraction to these stars does not entail any sort of sexual energy but rather social. They are impressed by a woman who uses her body the way she wants to. No strings attached. No social shame. And yet with Britney things seemed to be a bit different. If gay men found Madonna to be a powerful figure, could the same devotion be attached to someone as mouldable as Britney? For gay women, of all ages, Britney certainly was a sexual figure as well as a powerful one. Again, I am making assumptions. But it would seem to me that a lesbian interest in a star like Britney Spears would fall on the same plane as that of a heterosexual interest. Added to this would be a sort of admiration for a young girl, beautifully created, who had staked a claim firmly in the imagination of the youth culture.

What rings true for all of these demographics is the need for Britney to stay the same – young, innocent and sexual. This is true for any star and their fan base. When we meet a celebrity in a particular context, we prefer for that context to remain the same. But again, things are different with Britney in that we want her to stay the same, but we want her to mature as a sexual being. We want to see her grow but only in a particular way. We looked forward to her body development and cared less about that of her psychological state. Initiating the latter would have been an acceptance of Britney as a real human being. So the conflation of her as an innocent and sexy product is truly a fusion of our paradoxical permission for her development. Stay a child, become a sexualized woman. She sang about this for us, closing the deal with her song about living the middle ground between girl and womanhood.

But we forgot something. We forgot that along with becoming a sexually mature body comes the possibility of childbirth. The physiological and physical meanings of breasts, ovaries, uterus walls and the like, develop for a reason. Even in the twenty-first century, bodies operate according to design. They don't need to be used in this way, but they often are. Britney did it, used her body to create another. And all hell broke loose.

First, some reflection on physiology. The fact that Britney's body grew up should not have been a surprise to us. Indeed, we were waiting for such an event to happen. And while it may not have been a shock for us to see her body growing, it was the way it grew that troubled us. Or more strongly put, I think it disgusted us. The source of the grotesque was her crotch. A year or so after she gave birth to her first child, 14 September 2005, her crotch would be photographed for all to see. More on that later. Childbearing demands a great deal from the body. And while oestrogen levels, pelvic bone structures, mammary glands and other parts of the female anatomy change and alter to allow a birth to occur, the most trauma happens in the uterus and vaginal canal. It is a beautiful thing, but it is a horrendous beauty. The strong women I know who have had children have sometimes been fairly blunt about the process of giving birth, at times more so than I can bear to hear. But I listen and am amazed by what happens below the waist during a pregnancy. Stretching, cutting, bleeding, and then a life happens.

Our imagination of Britney's below the waist never made room for such metamorphosis or catastrophe. Never made room for such beauty and life. At first her sex was a forbidden fruit, tempting but not available. As her career developed, the temptation got stronger, more utilized by the overselling of Britney as a sex object. While we never saw below the waist, we definitely were invited to try by photo shoots involving bikinis falling off, jeans unzipped and opened. Her crotch, in a real way, became an entity of its own, a gateway to something unthinkable and potentially wonderful. In other words, it was unreal. This all changed when she gave birth to Sean Preston, her first child. Below the waist became a utility, a real thing, employed by Britney, for Britney. When this happened, when her genitalia became used, it became hers for the first time. And as a logical extension, she had the opportunity to become a real woman right in front of our eyes. As such, she grew up. Our stifling stopped, and her development finally made its debut on the cultural stage.

This normal development for Britney Spears was grotesque to most because it involved a tearing down of the infinite image of perfection. For Daniel Edwards, a sculptor from Indiana, the event of her having a child became something different. His statue, 'Monument to Pro-Life: The Birth of Sean Preston', pictures Britney on her hands and knees, naked, giving birth, the head of the child exiting her from behind. She kneels on a bear skin rug. Edwards was able to take the disgust and turn it into a political statement about pro-life. Apparently, the statue was meant to honour Britney's decision to have a child rather than continue her career. Ignorant to the fact that having a baby was going to be made part of her career, Edwards nonetheless moulds her body in a way that is analogous to all of our work on Britney Spears. Just like us, he made her what he wanted her to be – a political argument, a statue of objectification.

Statue and grotesque genitalia aside, the surveillance of Britney's body maturation and its twist from sexual energy to motherhood illustrates a turning point in the exiling of Britney. We could no longer use her in the way we had in the past; everything had changed. And when this change was presented to us we threw in the towel, and started our push against her. For the first time, she was being pitched by us and not her management. But our pitching was literal.

Not helping the situation was that she was a terrible mother, or so it appeared. Pop-culture media and the paparazzi love it when female celebrities become mothers. The tabloids are full of slender bodies now chubby, of no-make-up outings to the diaper store, of kids under newly shaped arms. The reason for their interests in these new mothers falls in the fact that they see the marketability of transformation. From small to big, big to small, toned to fat, the body becomes a silly putty which looks great on film. On a more pragmatic level, the monitoring of new celebrity mothers points to a desire to see what motherhood looks like for the rich and famous. These mothers become billboards upon which issues of child-rearing, morality and family culture get tested out. All of this is to say that when Britney had Sean Preston, the baby monitoring of our society was well established.

So they were there, we were there, when she almost dropped him because of a debacle with a coffee mug. We pulled alongside her car when she forgot to put the kid in a child seat. We followed her in to the Los Angeles police department several times, gawking as they questioned her about being a fit parent. When she and Kevin made fun of being 'country parents' for MTV, we were there, laughing but mostly cringing. On 12 September 2006 we pretended to be happy for her when the second son, Jayden James, was born. The celebration ended as we saw her filing for divorce two months later, again convicting her not as a woman but now as a mother. Then the crotch shot, something a mother should never do.

And of course all of the court dates, the demands for drug testing, the parenthood classes, the car accidents. It all was very un-motherly.

Surveying this course of events makes it all too clear that our shifting criteria for Britney was and is unstoppable. But the events of her motherhood, or more succinctly her performance of motherhood, also point to an uneasiness with her new role. On one hand, it could be said that Britney became a mother in order to stave off the cameras and the glamorous life – certainly Daniel Edwards saw this. Becoming a mother meant a change of venue for her body and her life. On the other hand, maybe it was inevitable that we, the purveyors of her young self, would never be happy with her being a mother. There was no way her abilities as a caregiver could actually replace her abilities as sexy Lolita. Such transformation is asking too much of a one-dimensional expectation. Stars are not meant to change, and when they do we often lose interest. Her management knew this, and in some ways, she must have as well.

But that doesn't really matter here. What matters is that it was hard for us to swallow Britney as a mother. We tried, maybe, but in trying we actually just found more ways to dig into her. In the end, it was our stubbornness that made motherhood a part of her exile. We were too stubborn to relinquish our image of Britney, too stubborn to let her be flexible, too stubborn to become flexible ourselves. As a culture that promotes singularity of identity, knowing Britney as both pop star and mother was too much. We put our foot down firmly on the line between our expectations and her reality.

The vantage point we missed was that of the kid's. We can fool ourselves into thinking that some of our distaste for her as a mother came from the fact that we were thinking of the welfare of her two boys. But I don't think that's true. If we would've actually pushed aside our stubbornness, stopped the race for while, we could have contemplated a child's vantage point of a loving mother. True, a mother who had a stress level beyond any contemplation or understanding. Furthermore, a mom who was forced to be everything for everyone. Among the celebrity moms, perhaps the Queen. Nonetheless, she was their mother. She was the scent that signalled comfort, safety, love. Her skin felt like security to them. Her body was their refuge. What we saw was fifteen minutes of chaos counterbalanced by millions of minutes of motherhood that were hidden from us, thankfully.

Sean Preston and his brother Jayden James never saw the music videos, never consciously listened to the CDs, never saw the fan clubs, never understood the money. When they saw Britney they saw mom. Something we could never do.

Note

1. For expert analysis on how women are sexualized in advertising through childlike poses and scenarios see Kilbourne, *Can't Buy Me Love: How Advertising Changes the Way We Think and Feel.* New York: Touchtone, 1999, pp. 128–154 on sexualizing through adolescent poses.

Chapter 13

The Vagina

It's been so long since I've been out on the town with friends. It's also been two years since I celebrated my birthday. Every move I make at this point has been magnified more than I expected, and I probably did take my newfound freedom a little too far. Anyway, thank God for Victoria's Secret's new underwear line! I look forward to a new year, new music and a new me.

I'm just getting started ... happy holidays everyone!

Britney
(Posted on BritneySpears.com, 8 December 2006)

The memory of the first time is elusive. I can't remember, for example, if I was by myself or with friends. I know it was in the living room, out in the open. I do remember my reaction, very clearly. Sadness. Nothing erotic, nothing pornographic, nothing pleasurable. For whatever reason, I knew that this was the end. But I also knew that this was a beginning. In many ways it was both.

Maybe you didn't see the uncensored picture. Maybe what you saw was the edited photo, the one picked up by most mainstream media outlets. The one that had a star covering her genitalia, a sort of enormous pasty. Both censored and uncensored pictures circulated highly among web surfers, celebrity gossipers and the everyday news junkie. Looking at both now, it is hard to decide which one is more offensive. On one hand, the uncensored picture screams of spectacle and voyeurism, a shot to kill. On the other hand, the picture with the star seems more obscene. Probably because there is pictorial evidence that more people are looking. The star is there not to censor, but to focus. To focus the attention of the viewer as well as the weight of the photograph itself. The uncensored picture was seen by the real seekers. The censored one was seen by people like my mother. Somehow the latter seems more perverse.

Roland Barthes has a famous essay in which he painstakingly analyses the semiotic and aesthetic elements of a photograph from an advertisement for Manzini pasta.[1] In just a few pages he is able to express not only the value of a specific image, but that of photography itself. He explains with eloquence the manner in which an image carries with it meaning, history, politics and artistic value. His analytical work on photography and images is hard to surpass. Indeed, I'm not sure even his work will be helpful in looking at this famous picture of Britney. Several things are different in this case.

First of all, the picture worked through by Barthes was an actual acetate photograph taken from a negative. The picture of Britney is digital. And while on the surface this may seem to be only an arbitrary difference, it is in fact monumental. Rather than light captured on film, the image of Britney's vagina, or labia to be more exact, is a conglomeration of millions of digital signals called pixels. You of course know this already. But have you considered the aesthetic, even semiotic ramifications of this? As a collection of bits, the pixels that create the image of her can each be manipulated individually – unlike the shadow, or the sunspot, the pixel can be remade.

Such malleability holds both aesthetic and semiotic implications. Digital photography itself has expanded the aesthetic perimeter, has allowed the photographer not only to be a capture artist, but also a worker of plastics. Photography now means 'moulding' because of the digital camera. This is not to say that traditional film cameras did not allow certain manipulation processes, especially in the developing stage. It's just that digital photography makes it so easy. Consider the fact that most of the images of Britney's vagina include the entire frame (Britney sliding into the car, Paris Hilton in the background, the brown leather car seats, et cetera) as well as a manufactured close-up of the genitalia itself, usually included in the bottom corner of the image. Such manipulation took maybe two minutes on Photoshop. It might be too easy for us to manipulate space and time this way. A sort of instant, lazy aesthetic is the outcome. With regards to our analysis of the famous picture, consider two more implications of the laziness aesthetic. First, it could be fake. Second, the original picture might never actually be seen. The natural and physical context of the image has been completely cropped, forever changed by mouse pads across the world.

Compounding this laziness is the fact that these many pixels can be sent to many people in an instant. And it is the instant that matters. The bits can be quickly shrunk down into a collection of colours and numbers that become air, almost too faint to be of any consequence. And without consequence we do not have ethics, thoughtfulness, protection or culture. One picture becomes 1 billion pictures. 10 million pixels becomes infinity. That's what happens behind the circuit board of a computer. On the other side, our side, the outcome is a collection of galleries, thumbnails of Britney. On our side of the screen, we notice that crotch shots are becoming the next trend in celebrity photography. Complete websites are devoted to them. All because some idiots were too lazy to consider their actions. But idiots rule the aesthetic. We've given them that job.

In addition to aesthetic conditions there are, of course, semiotic significances of the collection of pixellated information gathered by the digital camera. This is especially true when one considers the use of digital photography for pornographic pictures of women. It's not that far of a stretch to imagine a collection of pixels symbolizing, even signifying, a collection of broken bits torn off the body of an actual person. Thus the formulation of those pixels, the moulding of them, represents a sort of violence against the female body. Reanimating, reforming, all in the name of perfection and fantasy. And yet moving beyond this simple idea of pixels being body parts, it is necessary to understand that the pictorial power of the camera and computer is never autonomous. There is always someone behind the button click.

When looking at the photo of Britney's crotch, what can we learn about the person taking the photograph? Perhaps the most important question, the one most difficult to find an answer for is what the gender of the photographer was? My search brings up no identifiable photographer. But maybe it doesn't matter. Our knee-jerk reaction should be that this photograph was taken by a male. It sweats a masculine interest. The vagina is the property of a woman, but it has always (wrongfully) been the prize of a man. In that way, the vagina has paradoxically been a mythical possession of men. Think of any popular euphemism of the female genitalia that doesn't immediately indicate that the woman being talked about is property. Is there some innate evidence of a male photographer here? No. Indeed this could be a woman. I'm just not sure our analysis will get where it needs to go if we assume this. The picture tells us more.

Notice first the angle at which the shot was taken. This is a vantage point of either privilege or grovelling; we are either being offered a gift or stealing a scrap. The former is unlikely while the latter is expected. Also recognize the scene in which the picture was taken, notice the overexposure of her body by multiple flashes. The picture tells us that a group was part of the taking, not just an individual. Along with this group comes the cultural message of gang mentality. This image is evidence of the fact that when more than one person thinks something is okay, it is permissible. Or, was permission granted? Was there a sort of understanding between Britney and her photographers? Her posting from December of 2006 has been interpreted as proof that the picture, which was preceded by one less provocative, and followed by several equally naked, was a publicity stunt. I don't see this. But then again, why should I, I don't want to let the photographer, or us, off the hook. Instead, what I see in the posting is a girl trying to make light of something she would rather not have to deal with. What else was she going to say? What possible back route can be taken by a celebrity caught with her pants down, literally, on the cultural stage? For our analysis to work, and for this to really sink in, the picture cannot be just publicity.

Back to the photograph, and its messages.

This point of view tells us many things: that many shots were taken, and that this is only one of probably twenty taken in that minute; that the photographer was probably as surprised as we are when we first looked at the picture (if the photographer knew the vagina would be visible, the angle of the shot would have been different); that privacy means nothing to us anymore; that the mundane of celebrity existence, like getting into a car, can be the most exciting parts of our days; that digital photography has become a way inside a person's life without actually exerting much effort, both on the side of the photographer and the subject; that our appetites change at the click of a shutter.

Take a minute to look beyond the centre point of the photograph and see the whole picture. Most who see the picture will never do this, but it might help. In the version of the image that I am analysing, the one that offered the largest frame of reference, in the farthest left corner we see a clenched hand. Whose hand is this? We can never know, but what we do know is that it alerts us to the presence of another. And the significance of this cannot be understated: without the presence of this other hand, this other person, Britney and Ms Hilton do not carry immediate significance. Obviously the millions of people who looked at the picture days later add a cultural significance to these two women. But in the event itself it is the hand that does this. They are not alone in some parking lot. Rather, they are accompanied. For them, a sort of constant accompaniment. The hand gives us social context.

Ms Hilton offers further context. By this point in Britney's career, she is looking to be revalidated, reintroduced as a body and artist worth our time. Paris offers, by her mere presence in the background, a marketable quantity. She offers a stairway to the mantle of attention again. Look at her gaze, and wonder about the nonchalant look on her face. She is driving, or will drive, and thus is placed in a position of power and neutrality. The picture is not about her, perhaps for the first time. Is her gaze one of mortification? Is she embarrassed for Britney? Is there some shame about the company she is sharing in her fancy, Italian leather-clad car? Again we don't think of these questions, all we think of is Britney's crotch. And that's another fault of the photograph itself, or more specifically our ability to read (or not read) images. We don't look for depth, we look for substance and foreground only. We don't see Paris. Or the car.

One more context, a very symbolic one. At the very right-hand corner, slightly above the bottom of the picture, you see the warning sign of the car's airbag. Pay attention and all we see is a partial image of the sticker, a partial warning. We know that something bad could happen, we just can't read all of the sign.

Do we even notice Britney's outfit? The white lace that finishes the sleeve of her shirt, the black silk, obviously expensive, of her shirt? It's actually her jewellry that should be remarkable. Or at least deserving of some remarks. Her earrings and necklace are not especially flashy, they are not immediately recognizable as things worth a lot of money. At least from the vantage point of the photograph, these look, dare I say it, common. So common that when a viewer sees it, she or he is forced to project their own, common resonances within the frame. This takes on higher consequence when those experiences are intimate. The power of the photograph, it seemed, was not only primary (that of Britney's naked body) but also secondary (the association with other naked bodies). This is certainly the direct effect of the normalcy of the photograph. In other words, the lack of a pose by

Britney allows a voyeurism that moves somewhat beyond pornography and into the realm of espionage. Websites offer photographs, even video links, from hidden cameras peering in at women using the washroom, taking a shower, changing their shoes. These types of sites offer, according to the argument, a sort of naturalism to the idea of sexual pleasures. The voyeur feeds upon normalcy. And yet in this picture of Britney, it is the normalcy that brings the most staying power. The fact that she is sliding into a car, sliding into an everyday activity, wearing normal-looking jewellry and a fancy shirt, makes the presence of her nakedness that much more shocking.

But normalcy was never something that Britney had a lot of. From her first steps into the Disney studio to her slide into this car, the ability to be normal had always been subtracted from her life. Certainly she made this choice, encouraged by others, to be something different. And isn't this photograph simply a testament to that? Isn't it the logical resolution, or conclusion for that matter, of a narrative that began almost ten years before it was taken? This is definitely a popular way of justifying the presence of this photograph in our digital world. It was an unavoidable act. It was expected. Her music has gotten more raunchy, her performances had pushed the boundaries of decency and composure, her photo shoots had gotten even more risqué, more fleshy. This picture was taken ten years ago and just kept in the vault.

The problem comes when we recognize that this picture, beyond being expected, assumed and eventual, was also desired and demanded. In other words, it was actively pursued by the photographer, by the website junkie. The question of publicity even brings up the fact that it might have been desired by Britney's management. And so, the picture takes on a new visual contour, that of a hunt, a conquest. The central focus of the picture again becomes the nakedness, nothing more. When you tantalize an audience as Britney had done so well up to that point, that audience will be left feeling hard and hungry, hot and bothered, empty. One logical outcome of sexual dissatisfaction, of pleasure frustration, is anger. He is angry, the photographer. It comes through his camera lens, a phallic extension of his optic anger, our spectoral frustration. The moment of rape happens as the shutter opens and closes, and don't pretend it didn't. She said yes, but not to this. She had given permission to look, but not in this way. The camera takes advantage of her clumsiness, of her momentary lapse in personal privacy.

This is how sexual teasing ends up bad. And this is mostly true for our female star. The brokers of Britney had been experts of making this young woman appear to want sex. Even if they deny this, they are lying. Look at the first CD cover, when she was fifteen. On her knees, symbolically a position of sexual submission. Her legs parted underneath the miniskirt. Intention aside, look at the picture. And keep looking. A coquette veneer is in all of the pictures. They are invitations, plain and simple. And yet they are false invitations, they are 'just enough'. But they are never that. They are bridges to more pictures, alleyways into sexual fantasy, avenues into angry boys, men, women, girls. All of the pictures taken before the crotch shot were stepping stones to one final event, one final picture of vindication.

This is why we must see these crotch pictures, especially this one in Ms Hilton's car, as a real push towards the exiling of Britney Spears. But the photograph is only digital bits: it is the meaning we place upon it, the practice we put within it, that makes it a beginning to the end of this person. The picture is of a woman getting into a car accidentally showing that she doesn't wear underwear. But we have made it much more than that. The picture is proof of downfall. The picture communicates a looseness that we are willing to place on women who don't play by the gender rules of popular culture. Inside the photograph, all of our suspicions are met: she is a tramp, she doesn't know better, she's a southern girl growing up in Hollywood, and she is out of place. She can be dressed up, but she can't be taken out. She is the sexual predator we have always wanted her to be. She is, conversely, the sexual prey we have always wanted her to be.

But mostly, the picture tells us that she is ours. Again, the digital, pictorial capturing of a naked vagina, knowingly or not on the part of the subject, is for the spectator a permission to obtain. The flesh of womanhood is ultimately private, ultimately hers. And yet we have perverted and mythologized this portion of the body so far that to see this picture is probably not as shocking as even I am selling it as. Female genitalia may be alone here, for while the penis has been objectified as well (in pornography, for example) it has rarely been assigned the same social meaning or discussion. It does represent male power, but it does not represent the same mysticism, the same mystery, as the vagina. The penis seems obvious while the vagina doesn't. And so capturing Britney in this picture is, in some ways, about understanding the mystery of the vagina itself. It's just that much better that it is this woman's privacy that we are invading and articulating. Because we have always wanted control of her. We have never been satisfied with being just the onlooker.

This picture looks like a lynching to me. And I mean that in the most brutal way. This is the hum of the lynching crowd, the energy of the people who let anger and frustration become their pure catalyst. It has helped me to think this picture is giving off more than just a visual message. I have tried to hear the picture, to listen to the photograph. And what I hear is a mob. I hear voices which have gathered for ten years, first as whispers, the adult voices downstairs while the young girl tries to sleep upstairs. They are muffled at first, but as the young girl grows up she hears the voices more clearly, and they gather volume. Just visible over the hill, this picture now coming into focus, the voices are many. And they are singing a song of conquest.

Note

1. Roland Barthes, 'The Rhetoric of the Image'. In Nicholas Mirzoeff, ed., *The Visual Culture Reader*. 2nd ed. New York: Routledge, 2002, pp. 135–139.

Chapter 14

Disabling Britney

We know disability when we see it plain as day in front of us. We know the markers, the signs, the evidence of difference. The wheelchair, the oxygen tank, the headgear, the scars, the shaved head, the drooling, the loud voice, the quiet voice, the look – all of these call out to us and say, 'Something is not right here.' Signs of physical disability operate as a cultural calling card. They let us know the deficiency of the human body and operate as reminders of what healthy life is and is not. It is in this way that people with disabilities enter the cultural sphere, as evidence of something not meant to be.

To use the phrase 'people with disabilities' is really a stretch for most of us. The culture of healthy habits and obsessive exercise finds it difficult to see anybody with a less than perfect body as part of the crowd. Push further, and people with disabilities are often not thought of as people at all. In the culture of perfection, it is difficult to be identified by anything else than the body. Because of this, people with disabilities actually aren't that different from anybody else, for they too are being identified by their body shape, condition or tone. But it doesn't seem to work that way. The sexy, athletic woman is defined by appearance. The woman with multiple sclerosis (MS), her body different, is also defined by her appearance. The former is praised while the latter is feared and misunderstood. We have perverted the body in this way. The physical characteristics of our flesh become the manner in which we know each other, the way we communicate to one another, our method of acceptance or denial. And so when your body fails to meet the expectations of the group, then the body overdetermines the person. In other words, when the body is defective, the essence of the self is also defective.

This is not to say that the sexy athletic woman is immune to the objectification felt by the woman with MS. In fact, it is quite the opposite. Both women are shrunken down to the conditions of their flesh and bone. The difference comes in the way our culture values them. While using the same lens, that of body-centrism, the result of evaluating the sexy athletic woman is a positive appraisal, one that fits within the narrative of proper living. Under the same inspection, the woman with MS fails. She did not work for her body, did not expend energy to achieve her physical state. That's what the woman with the athletic build has going for her – her curves and muscles, even her tan, are desired and thus achieved. The woman with MS body is predetermined, fixed. Americans have really messed this up. The mythologies that run under the surface of our lives make us believe that the body of the sexy athletic woman is a sign of independence, of hard work. And that the body of the woman with MS is an outcome, a tragedy that needs to be sympathized with. On one hand the American hero, on the other the American charity case. Two women objectified, two very different lives.[1]

It should begin to become clear here that we do this to each other, we initiate the process of body definition, understanding and disabling. Several of my colleagues who work in the field of disability studies have articulated this process. David Mitchell, Sharon Snyder, Paul Longmore, Simi Linton, and a host of others have worked hard in the last twenty years to replace a medical model of disability with a social one.[2] For the past century, Western civilization has defined disability in terms of the *medical*, in other words, in terms of the ways pathological agents operate within the body. Cancer, muscular dystrophy, cerebral palsy, Down's syndrome, spina bifida, and the like, are seen as active agents within bodies forcing them to express certain physical characteristics, referred to as symptoms. These symptoms become the targets of treatment, the bodies expressing them become patients. The goal of the medical model of disability is to heal the patient, obliterate the symptoms, destroy the disability. On the surface, this might seem fairly straightforward, even logical. And to some extent it is. We do live with real bodies that have the potential of getting sick. But we also live with personalities, aspirations and the need for dignity. Note the following results of the medical model: people become patients, labels, conditions; disability becomes an unwanted condition; disability is disease. The responsibility of curing is not only held by doctors, but also by people with disabilities themselves.

The list of effects of the medical model of disability goes on, but for our purposes it is most important to see the inevitability of casting disability as something only medical, as something that needs to be fixed, as something unwanted. Thousands of disabled people in the last 70 years have fought for civil rights.[3] One of their leaders, Ed Roberts, trained by black civil rights and feminist leaders at Berkeley in the 1960s, argued that people with disabilities needed to become 'people' in the eyes of the public, as well as in the eyes of the doctors and rehab specialists working for them. Roberts inspired many to argue that disability is something contextual, something made by the outer hemisphere of the society and its values. This was the seed of the *social* model of disability that would be articulated by academics with disabilities in the 1980s. The social model of disability says that people are disabled by their context, by their surroundings. In other words, buildings without ramps, transportation without appropriate accommodation, ignorance in the workplace, stereotypes in the shopping centres, prejudice in the public sphere – these are disabilities. These are the locations, the origins, of what makes people different.

This is a radical idea, that disability is transposed onto bodies rather than essential within them. But it works as an idea, and as an accusation. And it also works on the level of mental impairment, depression and the life of Britney Spears.

Initially, the idea that Britney Spears is disabled may not sit well with you. Considering her as a person with a disability takes us far away from the normal classification of her as a body. Indeed, she shares the space with the sexy athletic woman – she is the cultural hero of body perfection, so how could she be considered disabled? In order to understand her this way, we must make the transition between her body and mind. This can be difficult to do because we are not accustomed to understanding her as anything else than her body. All of the Britney products are physical. Her music videos, the dolls, the pictures, they are all impressions of her corporeal identity. Even her music, the product that gets the least attention, is physical. If you listen to her recordings the presence of her physical self is incorporated into all her songs. The timbre of her voice is always tempered by breathing, sometimes enhanced for particular performances. This is true for artists like Prince, and even Elvis Pressley, who want a sexual energy in their songs. The body is thus present in a sonic sense.

All of this is to say that Britney Spears is a flesh and bone presence in pop culture, not a mental one. And so to understand her as a mental creature, like all of us, is in some ways to ignore the physical. All of our interaction with her trains us not to do this, but we must. If we can begin to understand Britney as a brain, which means understanding her as a person, then we will see the presence of disability. We might even admit that we saw evidence of depression long before 14 February 2007 when she checked in to the rehabilitation centre in Antigua. She would check herself out 24 hours later, get a tattoo and shave her head.

Before any discussion of the shaved head, look for mental illness prior to 2007. Such an investigation cannot be based on stereotypes or tropes learned from film or television. We will not see any crazy hair, spitting or screaming out of control. Disability will be painted with a different sort of brush as we look for it in the adolescence of a pop star. Two pieces of evidence come to mind. First, the ever-present, always plastic smile that covered the face of young Britney. It's odd to think of a smile as being an indication of depression. However, the ever present smile can be an indication of a facetious outer appearance. The smile becomes a veil, covering a kaleidoscope of stress that no ten year old should have to bear. And yet, when the cameras were on, the smile was on. The eeriness comes in the realization that the smile is the same no matter what the situation. Look at pictures from *Star Search*, from the Disney Channel and from other early performances – the smile is the same. Yes, this could be performance strategy. This could be a technique learned from a trainer, a manager, a mother. But just as this explanation is interpretation, so is the idea that the smile marks the presence of depression. The second piece of evidence for early depression comes in the wide eyes.

My wife has a tendency to squint her eyes when she is photographed. When she learned this, at an early age, she made it a practice to open her eyes very, very wide when the shutter clicked. The outcome is photo albums filled with pictures in which my wife, from about the age of seven on, looks like she's terrified of everything. Britney's eyes, all the way up through her debut CD, have some of the same quality. The difference is that my wife isn't actually scared of anything beyond not looking good in these pictures. My hunch is that Britney is in fact expressing some fear, but of what I don't know. Nonetheless, fear and depression go hand-in-hand.

So in the smile and the eyes there might be evidence of some mental illness early on. Again this is only interpretation, but a set of questions nonetheless that point us to an important trend in this pop star's life: the possible adverse effects of living in the spotlight. Again, remember the social model of disability. It is context that disables, not necessarily the physical or chemical make up of muscles, tendons and brains. So what makes the smile and eyes so important for us to consider comes in the question, what context creates them? Pressure from the family, from the industry, from us? The assumption of a role to be played? The constant attention? All of these things, and much more, certainly could create a pathological condition within the mind. Paradoxically, they also create a space in which such technology needs to be hidden. This is the mental illness of celebrity. The context creates the pressure, the pressure creates the symptom, the symptom must be hidden from the context for it to continue. Fame demands the cloak of health.

Now, back to 14 February 2007. When Britney checks into rehab it is not disclosed why. Speculation based on other celebrity life jumped to conclusions about alcohol or drug abuse. And certainly there were signs of both being used by Britney prior to the date of her signing in. Some journalists speculated mental illness, and depression, as the reason for her rehabilitation time, but most of these interpretations came a couple of days later when she checked herself out in order to shave her head. Her desire to have a bald head was somehow the linchpin in our identifying her as someone gone mad. Here we have a bridge between the physical and mental worlds, and our expectations of them. The bald head was a rejection of something, no doubt. But what was it rejecting? From the outside, it looks like a rejection of sanity. How on earth could you cut off your hair, your beautiful blonde hair, that symbol of all your sexuality? That was our question. Consider the answer from the inside. Could this have been a rejection of the pressure, of the expectation, of the cameraman? Certainly we can see this as a giant, bald, middle finger to her management, her record company, her family, her owners.

This interpretation doesn't work for most people because it allows Britney too much agency. And this is a great moment to point out that we practice this social action all the time, especially to people with disabilities. We don't want those folks to be empowered or powerful because that would break the pattern of comfort we all swim in. Plus, they are just too angry to be given authority. They don't know better, and they need us to tell them what matters. So Britney making a decision for herself is just out of the question. That said, the only explanation for her crazy action is that she herself was crazy. A person out of her mind. A person with a disability.

The longest rehab programme that Britney kept herself in was in Malibu. She was there for 29 days, from 22 February to 20 March 2007. This was an alcohol and drug rehab facility. Alcoholism or drug addiction is a disability as well. Again the spirit of American mythology rears its ugly head, making us see addiction as something purchased instead of essential. If you are addicted to cocaine, no matter what the circumstance, it is your fault because you took that first hit. Same thing with cigarettes, alcohol, even pornography. Unless somebody forcefully made you experience these things for the first time, it's all on you. And so when Britney was in Malibu she was working on something that was her fault. But by this point, we had already begun to make our assumptions about Britney's mental state – shaky at best. And so while she was working on this self-induced addiction she was also working on a self-induced madness. It didn't take us long to make the jump, from addiction to mental illness as both being things that she brought upon herself.

The self-induced trauma continued, filtering into her marriage with Kevin and her work as a mother. And we were there for every moment, offering insights but not comforts. Most of us watched on national news. Let that sink in … national news, as our country was fighting two wars. We watched as she fired a longtime bodyguard for failing to pick up a hat. This happened on 17 May 2007. We read on 29 May of that same year a letter written by Britney trying to explain her actions: 'Till this day I don't think this was alcoholic depression. I was like a bad kid running around with ADD.' Even she evokes disability to explain what went wrong. But the denial seems more important. On 6 August 2007, Britney is in a car accident. She flees and loses her license. On 9 September 2007 she awkwardly performs for MTV's video music awards. She is heckled in the audience, insulted by Sarah Silverman only one minute after her performance and ridiculed by the media. The pressure mounts. Too much stuff to repeat here.

The timeline erupts on 3 January 2008. After a short day in court, paramedics were called to her house along with the police. Apparently Kevin and she had been in a fight. When they arrive, paramedics find Britney, with her children, on some sort of drug. She is rushed to the hospital. Of course, all this is documented for us. Photographs and video to show her final and eventual breaking point.

We've seen this type of story before. This impression of mental illness, this giving of disability to one of our heroes. Margo Jefferson has written extensively on the topic of Michael Jackson, so I do not need to belabour the point here, other than to say that we as a culture punish those we praise. And the simple reason seems to be that these folks get to the point where they do not wish to say 'yes' anymore. And why wouldn't they want to stop? Why would they want to say 'no'? They want to say no to take back their days, their mornings, to take back some sense of who they are to themselves when no one else is in the room, to say goodbye, even to their fans. We have such a difficult time accepting this. But what we need to realize is that the enormous pressure of saying 'yes' all the time creates a space for lapses of cognition. Maybe it's not mental disability, I can accept that. But certainly it is an impression of mental disability, an assumption of mental illness. It could be eccentricity maybe even more so by the pressures of Pop life. Yet consider the fact, again, that this pressure can create pathological difference. If this sinks in, and we are talking about the contextual creation of a disability, then we are back to talking about violence.

We could get bogged down in describing Britney's illness. For example, one could make a very convincing argument for the presence of multiple personality disorder in the life of Britney Spears. Think of the multiple persons she needs to be in order to get through a daily routine. In 2007, she would have to be the following: a daughter to a mother who acted more like a manager than a caregiver; a client to many different corporations for whom she made a great deal of money; the estranged wife of a pop fungus for whom she made a great deal of money; a mother of two children, both of whom asked her to be something she seemed uncomfortable with; and finally, Britney Spears, the star. Of course we are all asked to be different every day of our lives. Son, brother, husband, father, professor, musician, cripple – this is who I am asked to be every day. But not all of these are public persona. Only the last three ask me to step on a very particular stage to perform them. The cripple is present most often, the most demanding performance. For Britney, all of her roles are major, spectacular, public. All of her roles are documented, photographed, videotaped for posterity.

This is the context through which disability arrives for Britney. Like a prejudiced society, like a stairwell in a public library, like a stare in a shopping mall, these are the pieces that disable her. And yet, it still can be said that Britney took a role in her own disabling. Certainly she is not a puppet, a completely malleable substance. Or is she?

When I was a freshman in college, I was eating lunch one day with two friends and a couple of fellow students we had just met. The conversation, as it often did, turned to why I was in a wheelchair. I answered with my stock answer: I was born with a form of muscular dystrophy called spinal muscular atrophy (SMA). The synapse of my nerves did not work correctly, thus the message from my brain asking my legs to 'walk' didn't make it all the way. I could feel my legs, but they couldn't carry me. I could move my arms, just not as well as you. Actually, a very medical model answer – what was wrong with me? My body.

The new people at the table, the acquaintances, wondered if I had ever gone to a faith healer. They had wondered, for some time it turned out, if my family had ever gone to one of those modern-day tent revivals were people with asthma are healed by the touch of some self-proclaimed prophet. I told them that we had gone to one service where they prayed over us, me and my brother who also has SMA. I told them, obviously, that it didn't work. And then I tried to explain to them why it didn't matter to me. Why I had come to understand my body in a different way than the folks under the tent. They looked at me. And then very matter-of-factly said that my parents had not prayed hard enough, that my own prayers must not have been sincere. I argued that this interpretation was ignorant, but they didn't hear me. They never do.

The point is, these folks thought and believed that my disability was my own fault when in reality I was being disabled by them at that very moment. Their insistence upon my own involvement with my muscular dystrophy worked as a sort of branding for them. It made them feel comfortable to burn me with the justification of causation. Comfort is the key here.

We are comfortable with the disabled Britney because we are not comfortable with a real one. Her mental illness, or impression of mental illness, is perhaps something genetic or chemical. But we learn nothing from that explanation. Instead, we learn a great deal by contemplating the fact of our own action – we disabled her. That way, she still belongs to us.

Notes

1. No one speaks more eloquently about the female experience of MS than Nancy Mairs. For an introduction to her brilliant work, see Nancy Mairs, *Waist-High in the World: Life Among the Nondisabled*. Boston: Beacon Press, 1996.
2. For more reading on these disability centred ideas please see Paul K. Longmore, *Why I Burned My Book and Other Essays on Disability*. Philadelphia: Temple University Press, 2003; David T. Mitchell and Sharon L. Snyder, eds, *The Body and Physical Difference: Discourses of Disability*. Ann Arbor: University of Michigan Press, 1997; Simi Linton, *Claiming Disability: Knowledge and Identity*. New York: New York University Press, 1998.
3. For a detailed history of disability, and the disability rights movement, see Paul K. Longmore and Laurie Umansky, eds, *The New Disability History: American Perspectives*. New York: New York University Press, 2001.

Chapter 15

The End of the Exile, 'Complex Shit'

The end of exile is usually death. A death that comes at the climax of isolation, a destitute movement into the unknown. It was unavoidable to contemplate our thoughts about death and Britney Spears, especially in 2007 when things looked bad. History told us that many of the same sorts of folks, similar celebrities in peril, died at the end of their dark run. Marilyn Monroe, Cass Elliot, Janis Joplin – all of them looked death in the face at the end of their exile. I will not go so far as to argue that we hoped for death in the exiling of Britney, because this seems so wrong to do. But I will say that inside the imagination of the public, Britney's suicide was certainly lingering around. Evidence of this came in conversations I had with colleagues about this book. Challenges to hurry the writing, before her death would come. Even more sickening comments about sales of the book skyrocketing if my theoretical and interpretive scheme was true, or made to be. This was hard for me to swallow, hard for me to digest. But I was not surprised. At the date of this writing Britney Spears is alive. And I'm glad of it.

But the living that she is doing, her current existence, is not free of the influence of exile. Indeed, I think we need to be clear on one thing: while death did not complete her exile, she is nonetheless relocated from normal living. She has been since her first audition, since her first television appearance. But now, the exiling is more finite, more sophisticated. Exile is still her state of being, no matter what sort of 'comeback' is happening for her.

A return to the metaphor of digestion and excrement helps us realign our current understanding of Britney Spears in 2010. We consumed, digested and now we have excreted. The excretion, the messy part, is where we are currently. We are wallowing in our own faeces, like children who don't know better. This is what the comeback really is. Any comeback in popular culture is dictated by us, the consumers. We can pretend that a comeback is the product of new visions of artistic quality, different packaging, cathartic visions of life that need to be shared, a reinvention of the artist. In other words, we can pretend that coming back is the result of the work of the musicians, the actor, the author. But really, if we are honest, we understand that the act of coming back is actually an act of welcoming back.

Again digestion is key to understanding the comeback of Britney Spears. If it follows that we have digested Britney, that we have done our work on her, and that in our excretion of her we have initiated exile, then our preoccupation with her as a by-product of us becomes a sort of fascination with our own creation. Fascination with excrement is not new to the world of art. The American artist Paul McCarthy, well known for his giant inflatable artifacts, created his piece 'Complex Shit' in 2008 – a house-sized inflatable dog turd resting in a field in Switzerland. A gigantic symbol of waste, this sculpture acts as a reminder of our unavoidable attraction to the grotesque production of bodies. But this is the by-product of a dog. To see artistic fascination with faeces on a human level look at the work of Italian artist Piero Manzoni, particularly his work from 1961 entitled '100% pure artist's shit'. Influenced by Marcel Duchamp's 'readymades', these 90 numbered cans of Manzoni's poop were priced at their weight in gold, eventually portions of which were sold for up to $35,000 at a Sotheby's auction in New York City. High culture, if you are comfortable with that designation, is certainly interested in crap. But not just for the spectacle or the absurdity. Faeces operate as art works among the philosophical tenets of the grotesque, marking a sophisticated understanding of how artistic expression and marketplace greed blend, as well as how human bodies become product-makers in a capitalist society.

Britney Spears works as a popular culture version of faeces art, especially in the context of her so-called comeback. Again, don't get bogged down in the details here, we are not working in the vernacular of the everyday. We are outside of the real, we are in the space of non-space. More on that later. For the time being we need to work with Manzoni's ideas more. The concept of collecting what we defecate, displaying it and then selling it creates for us a strange but illuminating vision of how Britney is operating today. Certainly it has been the argument of this work that we have taken ownership, sometimes violently, of Britney Spears. To articulate this idea, she has been painted here as foodstuff, as something to be consumed and secreted. As excrement she is not in fact waste. Manzoni's work opens a space in which waste is part of the art world. Put more usefully, waste has the possibility of particular value. She is not wasted, but instead useful waste.

She is useful in the same way that Manzoni's waste was. She operates now, in her comeback, as a reminder of what we have done to ourselves and our culture. But she does not operate as a result. Instead she operates as an active product, albeit a used one. We find ownership in her now because she has been through us. In an odd way we have birthed her in our bowel movement. Now everything that she does is part of us. When she had guest appearances on the TV show *How I Met Your Mother*, co-starring with the other comeback artist Neil Patrick Harris, it was really us on the TV screen. That's why it got such great reviews. We were acting, our child was acting, she was us. Britney Spears' parents had been transformed into millions of parents.

The same can be said, I think, about the grand reviews Britney received for her latest album, *Circus*.[1] Writers from several magazines and websites, all of whom joined in for the exiling party a year before, praised this record as Britney's most honest. They applauded the lyrics as evidence of a woman beginning to understand her place in society, and her family, in her own experiences. The CD has sold well, though not debuting on the pop charts where experts said it needed to. And while some of these positive critiques are justifiable, they also seem dishonest at some level. I think guilt plays a good deal in the positive review of this record – our guilt, our realization of what we had done to her. But I think the most complex understanding of her praised comeback has to do with our new feeling of involvement, of new ownership, in her pop culture performances.

This is a different sort of ownership than the kind that goes along with objectification. In the past, our objectification of Britney operated in a very generic way – she was sex, she was a body, she was an object. And while ownership had a part to play in this, it assumed a fairly passive role, largely because it mingled with other forms of popular objectification that have become normalized by our purchasing practice. Britney was objectified by a company so that we, in turn, could objectify her as well. This is how capitalism works when it comes to the bodies of performers. They are purchasable because of an innate system of dehumanizing marketing strategies. So when we bought the posters, we weren't actually enacting any sort of active objectification. We were merely buying into a process put in place several steps before us. But the comeback was different. Even though it is possible to argue that her re-entry into the good life was initiated by a company, they were also (perhaps more importantly) banking on the fact that we had become part of the propriety. We had become part of the shareholders of Britney Spears because we had digested her into her new existence.

And we love it, because she is young again. She is new, innocent, virginal again. The 25 August 2008 issue of *OK!* Magazine presented the Virgin well. Both the cover of the magazine and the initial pages of the article show Britney, with her two boys, dressed completely in white. She is no longer overweight, no longer droopy eyed, no longer shaven headed – she is blonde again, back to our comfortable expectation. The breasts are back, the smile is back. Hailed as the first interview in two years, the article reads like a conversation with a five year old, more specifically, like a conversation with a young Britney. One-line answers are given to mundane questions like, 'What do you do in the morning?', 'What are you wearing these days?' and 'Do you cook for your kids?' These are the types of questions asked of the exiled, the feebleminded. No questions about divorce, hardly any questions about parental rights, no questions about addiction. Instead, pithy provocations meant to avoid disrupting a sleeping monster. All the tough questions go to her dad, Jamie, who was also interviewed for the article. In the last couple of months of 2008 he was assigned the role of Britney's conservator, handling all of her estate and finances. It is he who gives the answers about Kevin, the custody of the children, and the emotional and physical state of his daughter.

Although he admits that she is still manipulative, the quote that gets blown up in big font is, 'God has a way a turning something bad into something good.'

A more realistic statement might be that *we* have a way of turning something bad into something good. We applauded Britney as a child, wrecked her in late adolescence, and now wish to cuddle with her again as a product of our own work and devising. She is in no place to do anything for herself. She is in no place, literally.

The writing of French anthropologist Marc Augé, in particular his book *Non-Places: An Introduction to an Anthropology of Supermodernity*, helps us understand the temporality of space and time in a way that points to Britney's current location.[2] Written three years before her debut CD, *Non-Places* helps its reader understand that contemporary life, what Augé terms 'supermodernity' (what most folks refer to as postmodernity), is filled with spaces that hold no physical or time-related finality. He calls these spaces, which include airports, shopping malls, amusement parks, etc., 'non-places'. What becomes fascinating about these non-places is that they are still enriched with meaning and value, just like other concrete places. In fact, non-places have become those mental and physical environments of our fast-paced lifestyle in the West. They are where we live, while never actually living there. These places are invested in and created by the mass media, television, cinema and digital technology. Understand that the iPod, iPhone and iPad, for example, create most of the aural and visual space of this new locale – the music and digital bytes of our earphones, the flat screens which we can touch and make move for our purposes, create for us the atmosphere of isolation and independence.

The relationship between non-places and the actual places of our lives is complex. It may be useful to think about the fact that we are always bound to our surroundings: our physical realities are always touchable, felt by our real fingers, hands and bodies. But the world that we live in is not only tactile. In fact, the world's presence in our life is only half-filled with reality. The other half is self-created. And this self-created atmosphere, this imagination of 'the world', is what we create via our sense of self, others and the communities we live in. These are the non-places that Augé helps us articulate and consequently study more clearly. The fact that new media helps us construct these spaces should not come as a surprise. Nor should we assume immediately that the media offer a negative input only. In fact it's quite the opposite. The worlds of film and television, of music and comic books, of novels and radio, of social networking, expand the horizon of our imaginations; they have the ability to enlarge our conception of each other. The problem is that we are only conscious of their influence when it is negative. And this is the case in their offerings of Britney Spears into our brain space.

As such, we have constructed a series of events and images that constitute the person Britney Spears inside the non-place of postmodern living. The media have helped us, but they have not done all the work. As we have discussed throughout this book, our implementations and permissions, our violence, our work has brought Britney to this non-place. And when we look at her today we must begin to recognize that she is at home in this non-place. But more harshly, she is a permanent resident of non-place.

So repeat the questions from *OK!* Magazine.

'What do you do in the mornings?'

We can answer for her now. She appreciates where she is, she notices that she is mostly alone, she contemplates a day spent in performance. This early morning process repeats itself every day in the atmosphere of non-place: who am I? Who will I be today? What will I do today? In the non-place she doesn't have to answer any of these. She has no effort to give, it is peaceful. She is us in the most complete sense of the word. And as such she need not be herself. We operate as her, giving her permission, denying certain activities, applauding others. All is approved or denied by us, her.

'What are you wearing these days?'

'I wear what my parents, my fans want me to wear.'

In fact, we are clothing. She wears us, her creators, wherever she goes. In the original article she tells the interviewer that she has found a certain brand of blue jeans that she loves – their fit is skintight but still comfortable. The closer the skintight jeans fit, the closer we are. Look at the fabric and see your face.

'Do you cook for your kids?'

'Of course, I have to. That's what I'm expected to do now that I am a new person.'

She is a new person only in the sense that she has been re-created by systemic action.

We are the proud parents of a new Britney Spears. The end of her exile is complete subordination to the will of us. And the beauty of this final submission is in fact the beauty of our own art, collected in the can that is the body of a twenty-nine-year-old woman. As we look in the can we see a reflection of ourselves, our own product. And this is the turning point of the exile of Britney Spears. We sent her on her way via photographs, paparazzi plotting and mythologies of imperfection. But we missed her, and needed to find a way to bring her back. The only way we could do this is to keep her around on a short leash. She is now finding her way through our new rules which are not actually that new. She's back, trying to fit in the mould of what Westerners have deemed appropriate for female performers. She is a mother who cooks breakfast for her children, she is yearning to be a workaholic again, spending most of her free time in the studio. She is blonde, well toned, well tanned, drug free, sugar free, Britney free. She is Britney Jean Spears again, working for us, working through us.

We exhale with contentment again. Britney is back, and so are we.

Notes

1. See Caryn Ganz. 'Britney Spears, Circus Review', *Rolling Stone*, 11 December 2008, http://www.rollingstone.com/reviews/album/24358115/review/24597794/circus.
2. Marc Augé, *Non-places: An Introduction to an Anthropology of Supermodernity*. London: Verso Press, 1995, pp. 1–18, 50–79.

Epilogue

Naked Again

I downloaded one of Britney Spears' new videos for her song 'Womanizer' from iTunes. I paid $1.99 for the video, it downloaded in 35 seconds. In an instant I had consumed the new Britney, comeback Britney.

The first fifteen seconds of the video find Britney in a sauna, naked. She is covering her nipples with her arms, and her crotch is hidden from us thanks to her strategic positioning. As the camera moves in from a wide shot, we note that her body is more slender now than we have seen it in a long time. Her hair is blonde (or something like blonde) again. A close-up of her face shows clean complexion, healthy eyes and the famous pout.

The next scene finds her playing June Cleaver, cooking eggs for her lover, husband? He is not interested in her. Instead, he is interested in his digital calendar given to him on what looks like an iPhone (in reality a smart phone made by Nokia), one of several product placements in the video. We then move to an office, where the lover works. Britney works there too, this time in a black wig. Here, she is the office playmate, a modern-day woman exuding power and sexuality at the same time. She dances with a bunch of men in the office.

Next scene, she is a waitress with red hair. Tantalizing as always. She dances in front of the men. Joining her are other sexy waitresses and waiters. It's the same orgy scene from her video for 'I'm a Slave 4U'. In the seven years since the original was released, producers are hoping that we have forgotten. Or they are banking on the fact that we will never forget. Now the video moves into a scene where she is a limousine driver, seducing a young man in the back seat while driving with her high-heeled foot. In one scene she crawls on top of the man, an image from her video for 'Toxic'. At the end they are in bed together, but she is not giving in. She is overpowering, she is in control, she leaves. The narrative is spotty, difficult to follow and really inconsequential. What matters the most are the vignettes of her naked in the sauna interspersed between these narrative moments. They are the glue holding together any sense of this text.

Even this nakedness is a re-performance from the 'Toxic' video. She was bedazzled with little jewels in this memorable portion of the video. It's what everybody talked about. And now, in the new video she needs to give us something to talk about again. Her producers know this well. And certainly she does.

On the iTunes webpage where I purchased this text, fans of Britney are writing reviews of the new video. Among the 1,300 reviews by customers, the following sticks out:

> okay, this is the brit I remember… I have purchased everything that iTunes offers for Brit, and I am happy to see her confidence back! Everything takes time and I love me some brit… kick some @ss brit!!! Love you so much…

What's astounding here is the word 'confidence'. Take it apart this way: note that the comment assumes that there was a loss of confidence. That at some point, Britney had a career that was guided by a sense of confidence in herself, her art, her life. What an assumption to make, one difficult after reflecting on her life as we have done in this book. Pushing further, what about this new video exudes a return to this confidence? Her dancing? Choreographed. Her lyrics? Crafted and almost incomprehensible. She repeats the word 'womanizer' 44 times (if I'm counting correctly). This just isn't lyrical at all. The content of the video? If you listen closely the song is about resisting a womanizer, okay we get that. But the video shows her flaunting her body for this womanizer? So the content of the video doesn't seem confident, it seems confused.

So where is the confidence? Maybe it is in her nakedness? There is a well-known photograph of Janis Joplin naked. She is wearing beaded necklaces, but her breasts are visible. Her head is tilted to the left, and she stares at the photographer in a way that I have always interpreted as being a sort of inevitable glance. Inevitable because Joplin seems to understand that her nakedness is what people really wanted. But not in a sexual way. Joplin's voice was her sexuality. Her body, and by extension her private life, were the things that people always wanted to know more about. So in this photograph she gives it to them. She gives them a vulnerability, but a crafted one. Crafted by her. She is giving it away. Hence, this is confidence made naked by the woman herself.

I don't see this in the video of Britney. I don't see this in her nakedness. Consequently, the confidence articulated by the fan on iTunes, by the consumer, is myth. Or better put, it is fabricated by the very situation under which it was offered. Within the context of this book, Britney's naked body in the video stands as a final symbol of the breaking of Britney Spears. After years of being consumed, after millions of dollars have been made from formulating a particular body, a particular mind, Britney is only able to exist as a prediction, as unavoidable. There is no confidence here except that which finds its warmth in the making of more money.

But this is a breaking that we have never seen before. We have redefined a process, just like we did with exile. The breaking of Britney Spears leaves us with no visible signs of breaking, no tangible evidence of something gone wrong. Instead, within the meaning matrix of digital consumption, the broken body is exulted as perfection once again. The breaking of Britney Spears might not have gone this way. Her downfall happened within the space of about eighteen months. Within those months she was divorced, arrested, criticized, satirized, abused and chewed on. And our consumption of her during this vacation from the stage never ceased. She was never left alone. This is the reason I say it could've gone differently. Imagine a life for Britney that didn't involve us. If possible, paint a picture of that eighteen months that doesn't involve the media, the paparazzi, the cameras, the attention. Without attention Britney does not have a comeback. Without attention, Britney is offered respite from her life. And without attention there is the possibility of healing, of change, of newness.

But this was not a possibility for us or her. The relationship had become co-dependent and messy. We needed her and she needed us. Contemplating this, the video and the nakedness seems inescapable. As our creation, Britney Spears is limited. She can only be one thing, can only sound one way, can only look the way she does in the video. As a creation, she is bound to her creators by an invisible umbilical cord of justification, worthiness and purpose. Without us she is nothing. Without her, we are nothing. Only passers-by, only onlookers. She allows us active involvement in the media world, and we love it.

It's left to us what we will allow her to do. What we will allow her to love. What we will allow her to be. That is the result of breaking. That is the outcome of exile.